COME HELL OR HIGH WATER

a handbook on collective process gone awry

DELFINA VANNUCCI & RICHARD SINGER

COME HELL OR HIGH WATER

a handbook on collective process gone awry

AK
PRESS
EDINBURGH · OAKLAND · BALTIMORE

Come Hell or High Water: A Handbook on Collective Process Gone Awry
By Delfina Vannucci & Richard Singer

© 2010 Delfina Vannucci and Richard Singer

This edition © 2010 AK Press (Edinburgh, Oakland, Baltimore)

ISBN-13: 978-1849350181
Library of Congress Control Number: 2009940691

AK Press   AK Press UK
674-A 23rd Street   PO Box 12766
Oakland, CA 94612   Edinburgh EH8 9YE
USA   Scotland
WWW.AKPRESS.ORG   WWW.AKUK.COM
akpress@akpress.org   ak@akdin.demon.co.uk

The above addresses would be delighted to provide you with the latest
AK Press distribution catalog, which features several thousand books,
pamphlets, zines, audio and video recordings, and gear, all published
or distributed by AK Press. Alternately, visit our websites to browse
the catalog and find out the latest news from the world of anarchist
publishing: WWW.AKPRESS.ORG | WWW.AKUK.COM
REVOLUTIONBYTHEBOOK.AKPRESS.ORG

Printed in California (USA) on 100% recycled, acid-free paper with collective labor by 1984 Printing: WWW.1984PRINTING.COM

Cover and interior design by Margaret Killjoy:
WWW.BIRDSBEFORETHESTORM.NET
Illustrations courtesy of Strangers in a Tangled Wilderness:
WWW.TANGLEDWILDERNESS.ORG

CONTENTS

PREFACE
by the AK Press Collective

WELCOME TO THE collective book on collective process! Over the course of the twenty or so years that AK Press has been publishing and distributing anarchist and radical literature, we've gotten a lot of requests for good, short overviews of topics that are of interest to the folks in our communities: anarchism, worker's rights, solidarity economics, and countless other things. We do our best to seek out books to publish or distribute that meet our readers' needs, but it can take a while to find exactly the right author or book. One of the most common requests we get is for a short-and-sweet introduction to collectives. Despite the proliferation of collectives and directly-democratic organizations—including AK Press—there has never been enough literature *on* collectives, and how they function (probably because the people in all of those collectives are too busy to sit down and write about the work they're doing!). So, we were really happy to discover Richard Singer and Delfina Vannucci's overview of the ins and outs of collective processes and to have the chance to put it out in book form. Their book explores the countless pitfalls that can prevent healthy collective process, while continually reminding us of the ethical and political goals that made us form collectives in the first place and providing us with solid techniques to realize them. As members of a functioning and far-from-perfect collective, we've found their insights incredibly useful ... and are pretty sure you will too.

Collectives are difficult beasts. The idea behind them is ultimately a simple one: a group of people working together towards a common goal, equally sharing in the efforts to attain that goal, whatever it may be. No one person is in charge, no individual's voice is any more or any less important than any other's, and every decision is a collaborative one, born of discussions designed to reflect the will and the wishes of each and every member of the group.

People, however, are complex, perhaps more so than we tend to realize on a day-to-day basis. In the multiple decades that the members of our collective have worked in community, activist, and politically-oriented structures, we've realized that we're never so cognizant of the immense differences between people—even those who share a common ideological goal—as we are in collective settings. In truly egalitarian settings, it's frequently the case that even the simplest, most innocuous of details can become a major point of discussion when we realize that we don't all see the world the same way.

Putting it in those terms sounds rather simplistic. Of course people are different; of course we all approach things from different perspectives. But the realization that our friends, our comrades, our peers, and our fellow collective members *don't* share the same basic set of assumptions, or the same set of basic practices that define what we like to think of as "common" sense is a staggering one, especially in situations where a great deal of effort has gone into clearly defining the contours of a shared ideological structure.

And, in part, that's precisely what this book addresses: what happens when we don't all see eye-to-eye? How can we work together to resolve our conflicts in a way that values every opinion and opposing viewpoint equally and doesn't discount concerns that we may not share as individuals? How can we hold people accountable for the things that they say and they do, without creating an atmosphere of micro-management or self-policing? These are tough questions, and ones that are best answered through first-hand experience and experimentation.

Collectives are also very much about compromise, which is something that we don't like to hear when beliefs or projects that are very near and dear to our hearts are at stake. One of the major misconceptions about collectives is that decisions can only be made when everyone agrees, or reaches what we call "consensus." But complete agreement and consensus are very different things. In a good consensus process, *everyone* has to give up some ground, and everyone has to choose their battles carefully. That's not to say that people don't stick to their principles and stand up for what they believe in, but if collective members aren't willing to compromise with each other and work towards a solution that everyone can live with, then they may find themselves in a three-hour discussion about a minor issue that no one really cares that deeply about. Consensus isn't about winning an argument, and that's something we frequently forget in the heat of the moment. Rather, it's about finding productive and workable solutions to differing opinions. It's also about finding a way to make sure that compromise doesn't mean finding the least common denominator or a solution everyone can "live with" because it no longer moves people one way or the other.

This book deals largely with collectives that work on a consensus model, but there are a variety of other ways that collectives can make decisions—always taking into account the need for compromise and discussion. At AK Press, we use a majority-vote system for most of our decisions. But we also replicate the consensus model in important ways. No proposal comes to a vote without a lot of discussion and debate. Everyone's voice gets heard and, in the process, proposals morph and are amended in much the same way they are using a consensus approach. And every vote is rescindable by a minority veto.

In part, our decision to use a majority vote model rather than a consensus model is a result of the structure of our project. AK is a collective, but it's also a business, and that comes with its own set of baggage. Most politically motivated collectives operate with a sense of *urgency*. As Delfina and Richard suggest, this itself can be used to undermine collective process ("People are dying out there! We don't have time for all this nitpicking!"). When you add "business" considerations to that mix, you have to be even more vigilant. Running a business, and thereby sustaining your project, adds another, very different level of urgency to your endeavors. Bills must be paid, deadlines must be rigorously adhered to, and permissible margins of error become much smaller. All of this can lead to short-circuiting democracy in the name of expediency. Decisions must be made *now*, which can open the door to many of the dangers outlined in *Come Hell or High Water*. AK's adoption of a decision-making process somewhere between consensus and majority rule is one way we've tried to mitigate such dangers. It also means that we'll sometimes make bad decisions that have to be revisited and revised.

Running a successful, or at least solvent, business also tends to lead to divisions of labor that can threaten democratic and horizontal structures. Every day, every minute, shit has to get done, and specific individuals have to be responsible and accountable for making that happen. The same, of course, is true of most collectives, but in a business there is often less latitude for *everyone* to participate in *every* day-to-day decision. This can result, intentionally or not, in the hoarding of the knowledge that everyone in a collective needs in order to make informed decisions (another "red flag" Richard and Delfina highlight). The trick, or art, of dealing with this is being flexible enough to build new structures that, so to speak, circumvent the possible circumvention of democratic processes. At AK, certain "big" decisions (such as what books we're going to publish) are made by the entire collective. Whatever can be delegated to smaller groups, or even individuals, is. And all but the most basic, no-brainer decisions are documented in meeting minutes that are circulated to the full collective, and thus subject to debate and disagreement.

AK probably employs enough checks and balance of this sort to fill an entire book of their own, but the point is, again as Delfina and Richard make clear, there is no fixed blueprint for any of it. Every collective is different, composed of specific individuals with their own beliefs and priorities, and facing different conditions and challenges. The important, and by no means easy, task is to keep the big picture in mind, the reasons we all are sitting down together, the reasons we've chosen this peculiar (and age-old) method of organizing ourselves and relating to one another.

The burn-out factor in most collectives is high—even aside from the fact that collectives are frequently doing the work of sustaining small, under-funded, and independent projects and businesses (which all have their own unique set of worries), the day-to-day realities of juggling intense emotions and constant discussion can be incredibly draining. But when we fail to adopt, and especially to *stick to* a set of best practices and guidelines to direct our interactions with each other within a collective structure, the rate of casualty increases dramatically. How many intelligent, motivated individuals have left projects behind because they were attacked, neglected, undervalued, or silenced in other ways? When we work to develop and sustain stronger, more egalitarian sets of processes to guide our interpersonal interactions, we help to ensure that our collectives are something more than a group of frustrated people sparring with one another. Instead, a truly egalitarian collective is a model of the society we want to see, someday, in miniature.

In the final analysis, though, whatever your process, and whatever your structure, if you've worked in collective settings, you'll recognize aspects of yourself and your collective in the chapters of this book. It can be a slightly uncomfortable experience—Delfina and Richard don't pull their punches when describing in detail all the ways a healthy collective process can be (intentionally or not) subverted—but it's ultimately a step towards recognizing our mistakes and working towards better processes in the future. So read, learn, and explore the world of collective self-management in your everyday life. And remember: collectivism doesn't mean constant agreement or homogeneity. Celebrate differences, and work towards shared understandings. Capitalism has been built and developed over the course of its long and bloody history in a way that keeps us continually at odds with one another, and yet, at the same time, discourages any real independent thought amongst the masses. Explode it from the inside by building better, stronger, and more sustainable and egalitarian structures in your workplace, your community, hell, even in your family. And be sure to document it all in the process, so that other collectives can learn and grow from *your* example!

INTRODUCTION

BEING PART OF an egalitarian collective can be a powerful and liberating experience. Most of us, throughout our lives, have been in groups in the broader society—whether in the workplace, school, or other organizations—in which hierarchies of authority, power, and knowledge are paramount. Each of us is expected either to submit—most of the time—or to lead, if one has made one's arduous way to the top. Joining a collective, on the other hand, allows an individual to pursue her goals within a common framework, and to help shape that framework with her own contributions. Members are in charge of themselves and one another, without coercion or enforced obedience, and they work cooperatively.

A collective is simply a group of people who come together to work toward a common goal, like creating art or music, organizing around political causes, providing services to a community, or pursuing any objective that the group's members choose as their focus. Collectives are often made up of volunteers, but they can also form the organizational structure of businesses. Because a collective is made up of individuals whose interests will vary, and vary over time, and because the membership itself will usually change over time, collectives tend to be organic: the group's activities and goals depend on the composition of the group at a particular time. But the main thing that distinguishes a collective from other organizations is that everyone in the group is considered an equal. There are no authority figures and there's no hierarchy. Decisions are made collectively by the entire group, whether by consensus (which means that everyone in the group has to, ideally, consent to all decisions) or by voting (whether it's a majority vote, a two-thirds vote, etc.).

The notion that there must be leaders and followers is so ingrained in our culture that some might think that egalitarianism just can't work. But there are lots of examples of egalitarian collectives, some that have been around for decades. Food Not Bombs, for instance, has been serving free meals to all takers and to support political actions since the early '80s. It is now is made up of hundreds of autonomous collectives all around the world. The famous punk rock club 924 Gilman Street, in Berkeley, is a collective that has been going strong for over twenty years. (Punk subculture can sometimes be a good model for collectives, but not always—a point we'll get back to in a later chapter.) The publisher of this book, AK Press, is an example of a collectively-run business. And although a collective is typically made up of more than two people, this book was written collectively, with both authors having an equal say.

In an egalitarian collective, everyone is valued, and everyone gets a say without having to worry about being overruled or ordered to conform to someone else's wishes. It's a heady ideal. At its best, it stands as a model for a more just and inclusive structure for working and existing together. But equality and fair dealing don't just flow automatically out of good intentions. Egalitarianism requires commitment and mindfulness from everyone involved. It demands clarity and the willingness to work at it, which sometimes includes hashing out conflicts and working out solutions to tough problems. When the ideal of egalitarianism is allowed to flounder, unattended to, it can devolve right back into the patterns that most of us knew in our lives outside of collectives: hierarchy, mistrust, looking out only for oneself, and sometimes even underhanded scheming.

While every collective is unique, because it's made up of unique human beings, there are some common problems, as well as common strengths, that we have seen over time. And in our view, they form predictable patterns.

The purpose of this book is to clarify some of the problems that can come up in groups that strive for equality and openness. It's not meant as a complete manual for how to work in egalitarian groups, nor is it an introduction to the consensus process. (For people seeking thorough texts on those subjects, we recommend the books *Building United Judgment: A Handbook for Consensus Decision Making*, by the Center for Conflict Resolution, ed., and *On Conflict & Consensus: A Handbook on Formal Consensus Decisionmaking*, by C.T. Lawrence Butler and Amy Rothstein.) Nonetheless, we hope that these pages will be of some use to any group that chooses to function according to the principles of cooperation and egalitarianism.

IS THIS REALLY DEMOCRACY?

DEMOCRATIC PROCESS SUBVERTED

CONSENSUS DECISION MAKING is often considered a kind of gold standard in egalitarian collectives because many people feel that it allows for the most autonomy and participation by all members. No one can be outvoted or required to abide by any decisions that she did not explicitly accept. That's a good argument for consensus, but there are also good reasons to choose some form of voting instead of requiring unanimous consent.

Some advocates for voting have explained that they did not feel consensus left enough room for dissent. It is fairly common knowledge that people will occasionally be reluctant to raise objections during the consensus process because they don't want to be responsible for blocking a decision that most people in the group want to reach. But advocates for voting have also pointed out that dissenting opinions are more often and easily recorded during the voting process, exactly because people are able to stick to their opinions without blocking the final decision from being made. With the dissenting opinion left firmly on the record, a group is better prepared to return to the issue for further debate or even at some point in the future. This could be important if circumstances change so that a different decision becomes more likely or applicable.

Both sides on this issue make valid points, and we think that adopting either method is fine, as long as the group sticks to the democratic principles behind the process. Differences in process are not as important as

A Guide to Subverting Collective Process!

Yay!

Try one of these options:

the genuine effort to make sure that everyone gets an equal say.

Sometimes, collectives that claim to operate democratically have really only adopted aspects of the democratic process while overlooking the fundamental qualities at its core: equality, respect, mutual acceptance, and an open forum for the exchange of ideas. For instance, a group might look to process primarily as a means of deciding on proposals—declaring, as a result, that all decisions have been made fairly and democratically—while it fails to encourage or allow the free expression of opinions. In that situation, genuine democracy has been subverted. Rather than being a means to ensure that everyone's voice is heard, the decision-making process becomes an ineffectual tool that leaves members feeling frustrated and confused. In a worst-case scenario, it can become a coercive tactic to shore up the power of a self-appointed elite.

1- pretend not to scowl when anyone raises objections to your proposal!

grr...

You

Collectives sometimes rely on the assumption that the group's process is intuitively understood by the members. A group might function reasonably well without studying the process too closely, until a problem occurs, and then the group's ability to work together suddenly falls apart. Attention to process is never more important than in times of crisis, but by the time a rift has occurred, it's usually too late to cobble together a set of procedures for the collective to follow. In most cases, the unequal group dynamics that derail a collective during difficult circumstances have been at play since long before the problems became obvious.

A CLOSER LOOK AT CONSENSUS

GENERALLY, A COLLECTIVE that operates by consensus holds regular meetings at which proposals are submitted and discussed. At the end of each discussion, the facilitator will call for objections; if none are made, the proposal will be said to have passed by consensus. But this process doesn't always guarantee that there really is consensus: a lot depends on the power dynamics that come into play. For instance, if members are individually approached ahead of time and persuaded on the merits of the proposal, that's a manipulation of the process, as it bypasses the open forum, which

is at the heart of consensus. Or, if an influential or intimidating member voices strong support for the proposal and exhibits annoyance or impatience with anyone who raises concerns, his attitude can restrict the free exchange of ideas and influence the final outcome. When that happens, the resulting decision will not have been made by consensus.

If some members do not have access to the information needed to make an educated choice but have to rely on the assurances of the proponents that their plan is sound, that, too, will essentially invalidate the consensus.

The issue is even thornier when proposals do not pass. In many instances, consensus is not deliberately abused but simply falls prey to vagueness and misunderstanding. For example, group members might believe that if everyone cannot agree on a particular outcome for a given situation, then the proposal that was made to deal with that situation should simply be dropped, and the issue will remain unaddressed. Consensus requires that all members declare the outcome of a discussion to be at least marginally acceptable: it should encourage a resolution to which all members can consent, not a form of resignation, for lack of unanimity, that leaves the status quo intact. If someone proposes a change because she perceives a problem that needs addressing, that person cannot simply be overruled for the sake of group agreement.

Blocking, the prerogative by one or more people to stop a decision that everyone else would choose to pass, is the one aspect of consensus that seems to be universally embraced. It does not mean, however, that one person can hold the collective hostage to his or her whims. Blocking must be used judiciously and not as a power play. More often, however, pressure is applied by the more domineering members of the group to urge someone *not* to block and not to voice dissent. Blocking puts one in the spotlight and easily casts one as a troublemaker, particularly when it means defying powerful members who have already privately persuaded the others to go along with their agenda. Members who have established themselves as de facto leaders (yes, this happens all the time in egalitarian collectives) and who may have attracted a following within

the group through charisma or persuasiveness, or by scoring impressive achievements for the organization, don't have to resort to blocking to kill a proposal. It's enough for them to display annoyance, irritation, or agitation with the suggested action, generating distrust among others. A persuasive (or feared) individual could destroy a proposal simply by frowning at the right times, sighing in exasperation, or laughing sarcastically. Clearly, this is not consensus.

Consensus is not just the end result of the group's decision-making process, or the part where a vote is taken and the vote is unanimous, barring any blocks or stand-asides. The consensus process has to be built

into the entire structure of the group or organization and form the basis for all of its activities and basic operation. This is true for all egalitarian collectives, even those who accept some form of majority vote in their decision-making and are therefore not strictly defined as operating by consensus.

The basic premise of consensus, and indeed of any egalitarian group, is that all members of the group are valuable, everyone's opinions deserve consideration, and everyone's input is necessary for the

group's efforts to proceed, in a spirit of collaboration. It's different from the group process used by conventional organizations in that it does not set up an adversarial relationship where one side wins (often the majority, but just as often the side backed up by the most authority) and the other side loses. In consensus, the collective does not hold discussions in order to defend a particular position but, rather, to arrive at solutions that everyone can consent to. In order for everyone to give consent freely, there must be no coercion or unequal power. Thus the absence of hierarchy and authority is not an added stipulation to the structure of egalitarian collectives but is essential to the consensus process.

THE BAGGAGE OF COLLECTIVE MEMBERS

MOST OF US did not grow up in egalitarian settings. Whether at school, work, or home, we each learned in our own way to navigate unequal power relationships. Some of us learned to get what we want by working the system. Others became adept at cajoling and currying favor. Some

concluded that it's less risky to let someone else take charge than it is to assert oneself and possibly make waves. Some learned to trust, others to mistrust. These habits of mind are not somehow magically shed when a person joins an egalitarian collective. The same personal styles that each of us adopted to cope with the outside world carry over into the collective.

If we join a collective with the optimistic assumption that egalitarians can be counted on deal with their fellow collective members fairly, and always with openness, kindness, and trust, we can be blindsided by the same bad behaviors we've had to deal with in other areas of our lives, where we at least knew to expect them. Collectives are not immune from underhanded tactics, grandstanding, bullying, or the willingness of some to remain silent as small and big injustices go unremarked. Sometimes the bad behavior that surprises us can even be our own.

This book looks at the less attractive underbelly of collectives. Much of what we write may seem to imply that people who scheme and intimidate to get their way do so intentionally, but that may not always be the case. People tend to act in

> 11 - never ever ever talk through your problems with other collective members, inside or outside of meetings. That would make you look **weak**.

ways that they have become accustomed to, sometimes without even realizing it. Some people are used to taking charge and getting what they want. Others might be afraid to stick their necks out to call out bad acts when they see them, or they may genuinely not perceive that there's anything wrong with someone else assuming leadership.

Because everyone in the collective is an equal, there isn't an authority figure tasked with keeping bad behaviors in check. It's the shared responsibility of all collective members to look out for the health and integrity of the group. If we look the other way when someone grabs power, attempts to unfairly discredit or denigrate others, or uses manipulative ploys, we are endangering the collective's wellbeing as much as the person whose ugly behaviors we're trying to ignore.

It's not a matter of assigning blame, especially since the individual(s) acting badly may be doing so without even realizing it. But it is essential that everyone work to correct power imbalances, fear, or mistrust in the group.

POWER SHARING

The Formation of a Ruling Elite

WHENEVER A CORE group forms within a collective that takes on the work of managing its day-to-day affairs, like paying the rent, keeping the books, orienting new members, representing the organization to outsiders—the press, for instance—and ultimately deciding the direction of the organization without consulting the collective, members should become very concerned.

If the core faction scoffs at adherence to established procedures or ridicules people who are concerned about process, claiming that they, the hard-working, indispensable backbone of the organization, are more interested in getting things done than going to meetings, there is no collectivism at work in the group.

Domineering people often seek to disparage or discourage sticking to a written code of procedures. This allows them to act without the group's consent but without having clearly violated any rule, or even to claim that they alone know the rules and have in fact followed them. Worse, they may force someone else to act according to their wishes, again claiming that the procedural code, which no one has ever seen, requires it.

More often, however, a lack of process allows self-appointed leaders to control the collective by attrition

12– unless, of course, by doing so you can sway the person into ceasing their vendetta against you and your righteous planning!

and default. The issues they don't favor are allowed to fall by the wayside, quietly. If anybody complains, these self-appointed leaders can simply say they haven't gotten around to a given item yet because, since they are running the organization, they are swamped with work. Or, they can claim that that those matters that didn't get done simply didn't work out logistically. How can the other members, who have been kept out of the loop of any logistics, claim it to be otherwise?

Whenever a small elite has been allowed to take over, the remaining members are left to function only as worker bees. The ruling clique may seek to consolidate its power by fragmenting the organization, so that no one knows what anybody else is doing except those at the top, who have to be consulted every time something needs to be done that could affect another subgroup or the broader infrastructure of the organization.

In some cases, members who have been cut off from the leadership may simply work independently on their own projects, using the group only for the resources it is able to offer. If that happens, the group has ceased to function collectively.

Except in organizations whose sheer size would make it impossible, egalitarian collectives require a maximum of transparency. (And even some of those larger

Remember, kids:

Collective process is the war of one against all!

Never let down your guard!

organizations might be able to foster greater transparency by offering meetings and information sessions through smaller assemblies or sub-groups.)

Ideally, each member should be informed about how the organization functions from day to day. Each member should be able to perform the key tasks required for the group's daily work. (In an ideal situation, members should learn how to perform *all* the tasks.) This might seem like a tedious process, but without it, there's no power sharing.

The Responsibilities of Collective Members

A collective requires the active and vigilant participation of all members in order to function equitably and collectively. Just as those who take on positions of power subvert group process, so do the people who relinquish authority and lose interest in the workings of the group. Because a collective has no bosses to enforce the rules, everyone involved in the communal effort has to take responsibility to see to it that the operating guidelines are adhered to by all. If somebody acts in a domineering manner, it is everyone else's role to call that person to task and ask him to change his behavior. If the group fails to do this, then it is failing to follow the principles of collectivism.

Domineering members may strive to encourage apathy and lack of participation, usually by keeping people uninformed or clueless about what's going on in the group. This is an authoritarian strategy (which could be unintentional) to concentrate power within one individual or small faction. When the majority loses interest in making decisions, the few will take that role upon themselves.

It is absolutely crucial, in order for the group to function collectively, that all members take an active role and keep themselves fully informed. Whenever we throw away power, there's usually someone around who's perfectly happy to scoop it up.

RED FLAGS TO GUARD AGAINST

THE FOLLOWING IS a by-no-means-exhaustive list of behaviors that should send up red flags among collective members that the group's dynamics need to be reexamined to ensure equal participation (and to stop divas and egomaniacs in their tracks).

These behaviors can crop up for a variety of reasons. Some might be undertaken deliberately to create particular outcomes, but many are simply the result of habit, frustration, or plain-old burnout. The very individuals who are responsible for planting these flags might be the ones least aware that their actions could be having a damaging effect on the collective.

The reason we list these red flags is not so that people who identify them in their own groups can point fingers or find fault, but so that they might become aware that the dynamics of their group need attending to. Intentional or not, these are behaviors that can undermine the group's ability to function openly and inclusively.

Group Behaviors:

1. Meetings are poorly attended and those who do attend appear to be sullen and bored, letting a self-appointed leader set the agenda and do most of the talking. This is a sure sign that people have given up on the possibility of having meaningful input into the group's direction.

2. Meetings are not held at all, or not for months, because of lack of interest. (Note: some groups get together on a regular basis to work on projects. These may count as informal meetings if decisions and issues are discussed in the course of the work. That's okay: it doesn't signal lack of participation.)

3. Someone or a faction denigrates meetings (boring, take up too much time, people have better things to do, meetings are for people who are only interested in process and not in actually getting things done) so that they are rarely held, are hurried, or are badly attended. As a result, one small group or individual can make decisions on his/her/their own without having to consult anyone else.

4. People walk on eggs for fear of upsetting the "leader." People chastise others for having upset the "leader."

5. Someone or a faction derides the idea of using a facilitator or an agreed-upon process, implying that "our group" is above needing all that.

6. Unsubstantiated rumors and gossip, especially attacking someone for being racist or sexist (hard to defend against) or for unspecific offenses, such as being "uncooperative," "unreasonable," or "disruptive" (hard to prove or disprove).

7. A sustained campaign to discredit someone, with accusations such as "thief," "liar," and "control freak" being tossed about without substantiation or clearly

trumped up (i.e., a person who borrows or loses something is declared a thief and a ban is called for).

8. A petition being circulated for members' signatures that vilifies someone. People signing such a petition without any first-hand knowledge of the accusations, often in an attempt to be helpful: "I don't want that person to destroy the group!" (Or to avoid angering the accusers and becoming themselves the subjects of the next petition.)

9. Constant shit-talking about people formerly associated with the group, even in a humorous vein.

10. Calls for banning cropping up whenever there's a problem.

Individual Behaviors:

1. Acting exasperated that someone would waste the group's time with trivialities.

2. Crushing dissent by fabricating distracting excuses or creating a smokescreen.

3. Trying to create a feud by consistently slandering someone behind his back or baiting him to his face. (For instance: is there someone who takes every opportunity to complain about the same person? "He/she is a stalker/a sexual harasser/a sexist/crazy/out to get me, etc.")

4. Using outright intimidation such as staring down, yelling, histrionics, or acting as if one is (barely) suppressing indignant rage.

5. Acting wounded or victimized when one is actually the aggressor.

6. Acting wounded or outraged whenever someone makes a reasonable request, like asking for accountability of an expenditure. (Extra-red flag: does this person consider herself to be so far above the rules that govern the group that she might actually be appropriating the group's funds or other resources?)

7. Making oneself indispensable by not allowing anyone to help or have access to the information they would need in order to help.

8. Suggesting (or insisting!) that fundamental principles should be set aside to deal with a crisis (or to appeal to important constituencies, like sources of funding).

9. Having no patience for fundamental principles (implying that they, or ideals in general, are childish).

10. Relishing verbal arguments with those less knowledgeable or more vulnerable just for the glee of crushing them.

11. Demonstrating contempt for other people's ideas or their right to express them (i.e., by scoffing, ridiculing, or belittling). Not to be confused with honest debate, which engages. Contempt only silences.

12. Controlling situations with fear by flying into a histrionic rage at insignificant provocations (i.e., a group didn't put away chairs after a meeting, people working on a project didn't call before stopping by).

13. Controlling situations with fear by predicting dire consequences. People who are worried or perceive an impending crisis are much more likely to succumb to manipulation.

14. Creating and spreading doomsday scenarios while setting oneself up as the lightning rod to deflect them.

15. Paranoia. Ascribing nefarious underlying motives to someone whose actions are merely uninformed or apparently innocent. Going on the attack is often the most effective way to avoid having to answer for one's own behavior (e.g., someone who borrows without asking the right person is a "thief" and should be banned; someone who adopts a dog and moves it into the space must think that the group's space is his own private home).

16. Creating self-fulfilling prophecies that serve one's goals. (For example: repeatedly stating that the neighbors are becoming less and less tolerant of loud punk rock shows.)

17. Flaunting one's knowledge (esp. of anarchism, collectivism, radicalism) to set oneself up as the go-to person for advice on how to proceed.

TACTICS USED TO SUBVERT DEMOCRATIC PROCESS

THE FOLLOWING ARE some common behaviors that can come into play at collective meetings and within the group whenever influential or domineering personalities attempt to steer decision-making. They are not necessarily ploys calculated deliberately to shore up power or push through an agenda, but they could be. People who engage in these tactics might genuinely believe that their methods, even if a little (or a lot) underhanded, are the most effective way to serve the group's needs. Or, as we stated earlier, they could simply be acting out of habit.

At Meetings:

1. Expressing annoyance or exasperation with a member's concerns, implying the person is wasting the group's time, is overly concerned with nitpicking over proper procedure, or is bringing up subjects that are not relevant. Equality requires that all members be heard and all issues addressed. No one person or faction can determine what is or is not important.

2. Insinuating (or stating outright) that bringing up problem areas or voicing dissenting concerns is disruptive to the work of the organization or disloyal to those working hard on the collective's behalf.

3. Expressing reservations with a proposal before it has been fully explained by the proponent, in an attempt to stir up misgivings among the attendees. The focus then shifts to a discussion of the group's anxieties, and the proposal dies without the collective ever getting back to studying the plan itself. (A good facilitator

should prevent this from happening. What usually occurs, however, is that the facilitator will simply let people speak in the order in which they raise their hands, thereby making any discussion, which requires back-and-forth exchange, impossible. The person making the proposal may not get a chance to speak until well after a string of misunderstandings, passed on from speaker to speaker, has killed any hope of clarification. The facilitator needs to allow two people who are thrashing out their mutual understanding of an issue to finish before moving on.)

4. Objecting to something that was never proposed. For instance, A says attendance at meetings should be encouraged by publicizing them more widely. B, who prefers low turnouts in order to exercise more weight in decisions, responds that people should not be required to go to meetings. Clamor ensues against the anti-democratic suggestion of coerced participation. A's proposal dies.

5. Allowing the group to reach a decision and appearing to support it, then quietly steering them to the next agenda item before they've had a chance to agree on a plan for carrying out the decision. Similarly, volunteering to make something happen without getting too specific, then letting it drop when the time comes to act.

6. Stating that favored projects can be carried out by only a few committed members, but then, when it comes to projects not so favored, insisting that these require broad participation, thereby ensuring that they will

become bogged down in the logistics of coordinating a large number of people and will likely not come to pass. Similarly, insisting that some decisions require broad support, rather than just an absence of objections, and may therefore have to be postponed until more opinions are heard, which usually results in an indefinite (i.e., permanent) postponement.

7. Scoffing, scowling, staring down, yelling down, sighing loudly, acting wounded, worried, impatient, or put upon, and walking out.

Within the Group's Larger Dynamic:

1. Setting oneself or one's faction up as the de facto leader by taking on the lion's share of administrative tasks, thereby appearing to be indispensable, and refusing offers of help, particularly when that help would make the helper privy to key knowledge about running the organization.

2. Hoarding information, especially details that are crucial to the organization's functioning or its compliance with important issues (like paying taxes, for instance).

3. Setting oneself up as the sole coordinator of the collective's various committees or activities, thereby becoming the only individual (or faction) to have control over the organization as a whole.

4. Setting oneself up as the sole person(s) who can act as an outside contact by virtue of being the only one(s) with access to all the organization's subgroups or projects.

5. Acting as spokesperson for the group to outside interests.

6. Making decisions without consulting the collective, usually by beginning with trivial matters (like ordering supplies), which gradually grows into deciding single-handedly about larger issues (like the direction that should be followed by the collective).

7. Scoffing at adherence to process, implying or claiming that only do-nothings are concerned about following procedures while there's real work to be done.

8. Treating meetings as pedantic and tiresome (perhaps never getting around to drafting or agreeing to a schedule for meetings).

9. Claiming there is no need for rotating tasks because the most competent people should do what they're best suited for. (Note that task rotation ensures power sharing—something that domineering members usually don't want.)

10. Claiming to know the organization's protocol (which is unwritten) in dealing with any given situation. Pulling rank (seniority, experience, or special knowledge) if anyone finds reason to object.

11. Insisting that those who do the most work in the organization have more say in decision making. Equality does not recognize merit or status: all members are truly equal.

12. Stating that in times of crisis there is not the time or energy to adhere to consensus or due process because the pressing matters at hand have to be dealt with posthaste. The domineering faction may then appoint itself ad hoc leader, doing away not only with collective participation but also with transparency in decision making.

13. Using the oldest manipulations in the book: going on the attack so as not to have to defend one's actions and creating a smokescreen of accusations to deflect attention from the issues.

14. Creating scapegoats or pariahs to take the focus off the manipulator.

15. Bullying, threatening, or cajoling.

16. Martyrdom: "After everything I've done for this collective, how could you question me?"

THE PARTICULAR VULNERABILITY OF COLLECTIVES

EGALITARIANISM IS BASED on the assumption that all members of the collective are making a good faith effort to work cooperatively, honestly, and in support of one another to achieve the mutually agreed-upon ends of the group. However, this expectation of good will can leave a collective particularly vulnerable to manipulation by individuals who might seek to use their participation in the group to steer it in a direction that better suits them or as a means to further their own sense of importance or control.

We are familiar with the coercive tactics of pushy sales-men: gaining our trust by empathizing with our concerns and assuring us that they are on our side, promising to help us by providing us—ostensibly at great sacrifice to themselves—with something we want and need. When we fail to appreciate their sincere and hard-won efforts on our behalf, they act deeply hurt and betrayed.

Most of us are wary of salesmen and may not fall for their pitches. But when we are dealing with a fellow collective member—i.e., someone who is committed to the same cause and who embraces our shared belief in equality and fairness—we are not likely to suspect him or her of ulterior motives. Moreover, if one were to express reservations about the motivations of a fellow collective member, one might be accused of undermining the mutual trust that is essential to the collective process.

Unfortunately, we have seen such ugly power plays and underhanded manipulation of the group's loyalties happen in egalitarian collectives again and again.

Exhibiting stress, anxiety, or grave worry is a common way for manipulators to exert influence, since most of us are conditioned to want to help someone in distress, and we may be so eager to do so that we will overlook other priorities just to ease the discomfort as quickly as possible. By appearing fretful at the possibility that something might not get done or put upon by having to do so much himself, a de facto leader can galvanize people to act without attention to previously agreed-upon param-eters. Similarly, such an individual might quickly silence dissent by acting hurt or shocked or by giving the ap-pearance that he is seething with righteous indignation in the face of a concern that has been raised.

The group's most common reaction to a faction or individual who seeks to sway the collective's will is not, as one would hope, calling the authoritarian manipulators to task, but gratitude that someone is taking on the difficult work of running the group and its activities. These members become complicit in the power-grabbing tactics of the self-appointed leader(s). Oftentimes, collective members actually offer these self-appointed elites their loyal support and become openly distrustful or disdainful of those who question the actions or authority of the leadership. At this point, the group has ceased to operate collectively. It has become, in effect, a private club.

THE PROBLEM WITH POLITENESS

POLITENESS, WHICH SHOULD not be confused with respect, consideration, and common decency (all good things), has always been used as a tool of oppression—for instance, to discredit political dissenters and protesters, who are characterized as unseemly and gauche by those against whom the loud slogans and street blockades are directed. The same tactic is employed within collectives to silence dissenters.

Collectivism requires respect, which means honest listening and consideration for another's differences and feelings, but not conventional politeness, which is just a veneer of agreeableness, often used deceitfully to conceal one's true opinions or motives. Politeness is anathema to building consensus.

The traditional Anglo-Saxon Protestant niceties, such as not saying anything if one doesn't have anything nice to say, never expressing negative criticism, and rushing to smooth over disagreements, are incompatible with working collectively. Conflict is absolutely essential to the process of hashing out concepts and plans. Ideas have to be thoroughly and honestly considered. Conversely, making nice when one doesn't really mean it only breeds mistrust. A habit of straightforward, up-front truth-telling encourages the group to focus on the content of statements made rather than feeding the constant need to try to ferret out the subtext of people's remarks: "Did she say that just to make me look stupid?" "What does he really mean by bringing that up?" And so forth.

An absence of conflict is almost always a sign that dissent, or even honest input, is being suppressed, usually by an atmosphere that disapproves of making waves.

A manipulative person will invoke social niceties when it's convenient, accusing anybody who raises questions of being disrespectful or disruptive as means to silence them.

Politeness gives bullies free rein, since the social compact says we should respond with quiet composure to someone who attempts to intimidate us by shouting us down. Anyone who responds in kind to verbal attacks is subjected to the group's censure for escalating rather than defusing the hostilities, yet the original attacker, if he or she is a habitual bully who has earned a position of power and deference in the collective through domineering behavior, will get off scot-free. People may even come to his or her defense for being so put upon and vilify whoever dared to confront such a beloved and respected member. This behavior is more characteristic of a club led by a charismatic personality than an egalitarian collective, yet something very similar to this happens time and time again in groups that say they operate by the principles of egalitarianism.

It is essential for members to hear and consider the content of a grievance, even if it is delivered in a flash of anger. In a collective where there is an atmosphere of intimidation, which can be expressed as an insistence on social niceties and decorum, members who may have concerns will routinely keep their mouths shut. Issues might rise to the surface only when someone has been pushed to the limit and blurts out his reservations by yelling. When that happens, it's very easy for the domineering person(s) to paint the complainer as "crazy" or "out to get me." In fact, a particularly sneaky control freak may intentionally bait the person whom she sees as a threat to her power just to get a heated reaction, which she can then sell to the group as a reason to expel the dissenter.

Speaking honestly will oftentimes raise someone's hackles. The group has to create a safe and open environment in which this is okay.

There is a misconception that because collectivism is based on honesty, equality, and shared ideals, group dynamics will always be loving and supportive. The opposite is true. Collectivism actually allows people to give voice to their dissent, which can sometimes happen in ways that are not pretty.

A collective that indulges in bland expressions of insincere

affection or empathy and frowns on displays of grumpiness, anger, or dislike of another person or idea is not operating by the basic premise of mutual respect. Egalitarianism requires that everyone be given room to vent, for better or worse. Otherwise, there's an authoritarian premise at work in the group.

People get angry. People get frustrated, fed up, confused, defeated, vindictive, resentful, spiteful, and so on. The collective must let them be, give them the chance to blow off steam, and, if appropriate, allow them to apologize later.

Collectives in the U.S. often voice concern for respecting the values and priorities of oppressed groups and other cultures, yet when it comes to the personal interactions of group members, in and out of meetings, they often judge and condemn individual behavior by the most White-Anglo-Saxon standard of all: don't show emotion, don't raise your voice, don't lose control of your temper. And if you do any of those things, then you lose your ability to be heard or listened to. That is not a respectful or egalitarian premise.

Angry outbursts are only a passing storm, not an indication that someone is unacceptable or fundamentally bad in some way.

A single bad act or angry invective can become a tool wielded as proof of someone's lack of fitness to participate

in the group. Even some slight loss of composure can become blown out of proportion through re-telling, and sometimes outright lying, about what happened. It's important to guard against the notion that some isolated action or event is somehow indicative of a person's entire character. This is a common ploy: seize upon a molehill and turn it into a mountain to prove a personal agenda.

There is, however, a very important caveat to this issue. It's crucial to distinguish between an angry outburst that spills out from frustration and strong emotions, on the one hand, and, on the other, yelling and histrionics that are used as an authoritarian ploy to frighten potential dissenters.

It might not always be easy to tell the difference, but there is one critical consideration: does the person doing the yelling have any power? If the group's de facto leader habitually shouts people down, or appears to seethe with disapproval or suppressed rage when something is brought up that is not to her liking, that should raise red flags. On the other hand, when a member who is not particularly popular loses his temper, it's unlikely that he is intentionally trying to sway the group. Someone whose ideas are frequently dismissed and who doesn't carry much weight in the group knows that he isn't likely to persuade anyone with an angry outburst. Anger from a person in his position is only going to be met with scorn and eye-rolling, at best, or even expulsion as an undesirable element.

Collective members have a responsibility to determine whether anger is being deliberately used as a tool of intimidation, and if so, then the person engaging in intimidation should be called to task. That, however, is not easily done if the individual in question is deferred to by the group and considered indispensable. Anyone who publicly questions his or her actions is likely to find himself alone and ostracized for having dared to offend such a venerated member.

THE NEED FOR KINDNESS

ALTHOUGH COLLECTIVE MEMBERS should not subject one another to fake sentimentality and cloying praise, the shared effort of being in a collective presupposes good will and genuine consideration for each person involved. If the basis for interactions among the group is not kindness, tolerance, and acceptance in spite of unavoidable flaws, then there is a dynamic at work which does not support egalitarianism. The basis for egalitarianism is not shared decision making (that's an outcome), but fundamental respect for the concerns of each member and for the person herself or himself. Whenever there is bullying, ridiculing, or grandstanding, there is no equality.

In "The Problem with Politeness" we stress the need to allow members to express anger and other unpleasant or difficult emotions and opinions. It's okay for a member to be angry, annoyed, or wrong. People make mistakes; the collective should consider that a normal part of functioning. Those who commit blunders should strive to correct them and then move on. What is not okay is bad behavior that is intentional: that is, it has been devised to create a particular outcome, whether it's to intimidate dissenters, prove a point, or demonstrate one's supremacy in a given area. It's also not okay to upset other people just to amuse oneself.

Even those of us who elect to participate in egalitarian collectives have been living in a society that places people in positions of authority and submission with respect to one another. Most of us understand that equality means neither giving nor taking orders and rejecting any form of established hierarchy, but when it comes to informal hierarchies, collective members sometimes fall back onto what they've been accustomed to by mainstream culture. For instance, if someone seems particularly knowledgeable in a given area and willing to take on high-visibility tasks, he is sometimes allowed to attain a position of informal leadership. What makes this possible (in addition to garden-variety laziness) is the mainstream notion—especially difficult to shake among those of us who took pride in doing well in school and being recognized for it—that people should be praised and acknowledged for their talents and successes. In a truly egalitarian group, everybody contributes according to his or her ability and availability, and no one expects to get or take credit for his achievements. Hero worship is incompatible with egalitarianism. All accomplishments are built on someone else's shoulders.

Loyalty, which on its face might seem like a good thing, has no place in egalitarian collectives that strive to be fair to all members. Loyalty is what causes us to stick up for someone close to us, even to the detriment of another, when we know our crony is wrong. Or to overlook facts and forego investigating a matter even when it would mean clearing an innocent person of wrongdoing. Fairness requires that we listen to all and consider all possibilities before arriving at an opinion.

CREATING PARIAHS

ONE OF THE ugliest and most reprehensible tendencies that we've seen in egalitarian collectives is the creation of pariahs: a small group decides that some individual is undesirable, then he is singled out for vilification and possible expulsion. This practice might seem odd for groups supposedly founded on equality, mutual respect, and acceptance, but it happens remarkably often.

The basis for collectives founded on equality is that people have the right to be themselves, regardless of whether their attitudes make them popular or not. That is not to say that members have to accept being mistreated by boors. If somebody is bothered, she should let the offender know that such behavior is bothersome and ask that it change. It may not, in fact, change, in which case these two people simply must find a way to put up with each other. Human interactions are rarely perfect. It's normal for people sometimes to be obnoxious or awkward.

What so often happens, however, is that one or both people will make a huge case of the issue, start slinging accusations fast and loose, and demand that the collective intervene to remove the supposed culprit. It is not uncommon for members to be sleazily manipulated so that one side might gain advantage over the other. A hapless person who wouldn't think of devising strategies or masterminding plots may suddenly find that she is universally hated, perhaps without even knowing why. Sometimes secret meetings are held, without the knowledge of the accused, at which the attendees will hatch a plan to ostracize her. Usually, this is done for no other reason than that the complainants are too cowardly to confront the person directly and simply ask her to alter her demeanor.

Many times a person who is expelled does not even know what he has done wrong and might very well have corrected himself if only he'd been told about the offending behavior. Too often groups gang up against someone only because he has awkward social skills and unwittingly comes off as impolite or bossy. Do we need to say that this does not constitute egalitarianism? We've seen junior high students who behave more maturely.

An uglier form of creating pariahs occurs when a domineering member or faction intentionally seeks to discredit and eject someone whom they consider a threat to their hegemony. Sometimes, someone is targeted this way after she has been outspoken in condemning the control that the self-appointed elite has wrested from the collective. In other cases, however, the targeted person may have merely insisted that the group follow proper democratic procedure. If taken seriously, that recommendation might have the potential of removing power from the leading faction—therefore, it must be suppressed.

The easiest way to impeach the credibility of a dissenter is to accuse him of having a personal grudge against the person he is calling to task. The manipulator can then bait the dissenter with personal insults, and if the poor soul is ruffled and responds in kind, our Machiavelli will have proven her case: "See? He is just out to get revenge on me—that's what all of this has been about!"

There is never a wrong time to call into question someone's actions as they relate to the integrity of the collective's process. In fact, it is every member's responsibility to do so if and when he feels the situation calls for it. Unfortunately, few people ever do. People find it easier not to stick their necks out to speak out on what they think is right. They may even join in the condemnation of a dissenter, because they don't like to have their little bubble jostled. They may readily agree that the troublemaker is not raising an issue but making a personal attack. An egalitarian group cannot operate in such an atmosphere. It's likely that anyone who makes waves under these circumstances will find himself out the door.

It is the responsibility of all collective members to listen carefully and consider every matter that is brought to their attention, and to hear from all sides. Members should assume that every concern is sincere and treat it as such, but, particularly when one person's concern involves condemning another individual, everyone in the collective has to make every effort to get to the bottom of the issue without jumping to conclusions. Ask questions. Investigate. Look to possible motives to help you ferret out the truth. This is almost never done. People are usually all too happy to jump on a bandwagon of character assassination and are unlikely to be dissuaded from whatever stance they have chosen.

In cases of outright nastiness or bullying, it's appropriate for the collective to help address the behavior (although it still does not mean the offender should be summarily expelled!). Rarely, however, does the group come to the defense of an aggrieved member. As long as group censure consists of dumping on an unpopular person, especially if it's by e-mail or out of the individual's earshot, then people gleefully jump in. But when it comes to confronting a bully, then—poof!—everyone disappears. Even if the bully has been, until that point, generally acknowledged as such, when somebody actually asks for help in calling her to task, suddenly nobody remembers having had any problems with her.

Too often, ugly banishments happen because the collective has no guidelines for dealing with disagreement or dissent. In the absence of a grievance procedure or a forum in which differences of opinion may be openly discussed, the only options for the group are either trudging along in some unstructured, undefined manner, with everybody swallowing whatever concerns they may have and silently suffering any insults, or forcibly expelling whoever brings up a problem. In such situations, the promise of inclusion and openness intrinsic to an egalitarian group has been subverted and narrowed down to Shut Up or Get Out.

Sometimes, however, even when it seems that the right rules and guidelines are in place, these can be ignored or rendered useless. Especially in a smaller group, it is not all that uncommon for the rules to be overtly disregarded as members decide that those regulations are nothing more than technical trivialities. Thus, regardless of the rules, the individual who has been vilified or ousted has little recourse when the whole small gang (which might call itself a collective) has simply turned against her. Almost inevitably, she will end up giving up the struggle because it just doesn't seem worth it to dredge up rules that nobody cares about, simply to remain among people who obviously don't want her around.

Established rules can also be easily subverted through the usual techniques of manipulation, as described in other chapters. A group might earnestly intend to follow the established procedures for exploring grievances or granting due process, yet those procedures will become irrelevant if the whole collective has already been convinced of the accused person's guilt. Unchecked binges of character assassination and rumor mongering can psychologically nullify many "fair trials" before they ever happen.

Ironically, some people use the belief in anarchism as their excuse to flagrantly ignore rules that were designed to ensure fairness and democracy. Anarchists who break the rules might go on the defensive by saying that they don't always have to follow the law, because they are anarchists. Yet, while it may be true that anarchists can reserve the right to reject laws that they think are unjust or are the product of an unjust system, anarchists must also reach a collective understanding about basic democratic principles.

Rules can become very important, not simply because they are the rules, but because they can serve as guidelines for achieving democracy. Those guidelines might be very much needed during harsh or complex conflicts, when people are more easily confused or misled into forgetting the most basic principles or even basic logic.

Perhaps someday, everyone will have a strong enough conviction in—and knowledge of—true democratic principles never to be misled (or to do the misleading, for that matter). In some future golden age, perhaps, everybody will be so psychologically and socially advanced that it will simply be unthinkable—and impossible—for them to contribute to the creation of pariahs or other acts of collective injustice. Yet, in the here and now, we probably should do everything we can to keep those tendencies in check.

GOOD-FAITH AND BAD-FAITH CHARACTER ASSASSINATIONS

A CAMPAIGN OF character assassination aimed at distancing and ultimately removing someone from the collective can be undertaken in either good faith or bad faith. We're not suggesting that a good-faith character assassination is somehow good, of course. Both kinds are awful, but the differences bear describing.

The important distinction lies in the underlying motive. When a group targets someone for removal in good faith, they are doing so because they are so fed up, and have become so convinced of the offender's irredeemable undesirability, that they have come to believe that removing her is the only option. In a bad-faith character assassination, a faction or person intentionally seeks to get rid of a perceived rival or threat, who may not in fact have done anything wrong. The instigator(s) will deliberately scheme to paint her as "crazy" or harmful to the collective in some way, and will work tirelessly, and usually effectively, to convince the membership that she simply has to go.

In the case of a bad-faith witch hunt, only the original schemer or his close associates are acting in bad faith. The rest of the group is simply deceived into believing that the accused is harming the collective, and they join in to tar and feather that person for what they believe to be the good of the group.

In a good-faith instance of character assassination, people typically feel they have reached the end of their rope. Someone has tried their patience, or they perceive that he has tried someone else's patience, to such an extent that they don't know what else to do. Sometimes, there are only a few who have borne the brunt of dealing with a difficult personality or situation, maybe with little or no help from the rest of the membership. When things have come to a head and the beleaguered few want the perceived culprit gone, they may be appalled or outraged at anyone who does not instantly support them. They may see themselves as the hardworking and uncomplaining backbone, which deserves a little consideration now and then. And many of the members may agree, perhaps out of guilt. But should they go along with a personal vilification and expulsion just to be supportive? Ultimately, that sort of strategy will prove to be much more destructive than supportive, assuming people are still concerned about the integrity of the group.

Another, slightly worse, form of good-faith effort to remove a member of the collective happens when a small group, usually a faction having some degree of power, cannot accept a viewpoint other than their own. Anyone who disagrees with their chosen course is seen as a deliberate obstacle or saboteur. If efforts to control and direct that person fail, then the person becomes unwanted, and the complaints against him may soon reach such a shrill pitch that the whole group finds they can no longer stand having him around.

In a typical bad-faith character assassination, on the other hand, a domineering member or faction intentionally cracks down on a person they consider an obstacle to their agenda or a threat to their power. Someone may be targeted precisely because he has made some mild attempt to point out that a self-appointed cabal has wrested control from the collective. Or the reviled person could simply have been singled out for obtusely insisting on democratic process—which, if carried out, would have the effect of stripping the self-appointed leadership of its authority.

This type of situation is especially tangled and difficult to come to grips with. The majority of the members are, in this case, victims of the instigator's deception, but they are not without fault. If they were being vigilant about not jumping to conclusions, or if they refused to accept nasty allegations about another person on faith, they might be in a position to put and end to the injustice, or at the very least see through it. Just because a powerful or influential person in the group is telling you that something is so, you cannot assume it's the truth: you still have a responsibility to look into it and verify what she is saying by *talking to the accused directly*. And if you have not yet had the opportunity to find out for yourself, your responsibility is to reserve judgment until you can be sure of the facts.

If you are asked to join in malicious gossip or sign a petition that makes statements against someone or calls for his expulsion or some other limitation of his freedoms, it is your responsibility to say no until you can be sure in your knowledge of the situation. Especially if the issue is expulsion, it is better to err in pursuit of fairness. This may not always be easy, because the pressure might be great, especially if the person making the accusations has a de facto leadership position and is not often crossed.

One of the especially difficult aspects of recognizing a bad-faith character assassination is that people might be disinclined to believe that the instigator could be so nefarious. Ironically, the more underhanded someone's behavior, the more likely she is to get away with it, because people will simply not believe that she would sink so low or could be acting so maliciously.

On the plus side, the way to address either bad-faith or good-faith character assassinations is essentially the same, so it may not entirely matter whether they are identified as one or the other. There's no substitute for the painstaking work of finding out the truth and urging everyone to withhold judgment until all sides have been heard. We are not suggesting, though, that if someone is identified as stirring up a witch hunt or participating in one, she should then become the target of the group's condemnation. Whenever a problem behavior exists or is perceived within the group, it simply needs to be addressed. This might amount to nothing more than discussing the issue(s) or grievance(s) and reaching solutions that everyone can agree on. Rarely is expulsion the only viable solution.

It's worth noting that not everyone who is driven out of a group is forcibly expelled. Many more merely leave on their own, tired of the abuse or simply disillusioned. When a group allows that to happen, it is no less reprehensible than an outright expulsion. For most purposes, it's the same thing. The difference is that the conniving leadership—and the complicit collective—are even less likely to be exposed for what they truly represent: the corruption of egalitarianism and the creation of coercive hierarchy.

BANNING

PEOPLE IN THE activist community are often very committed to anti-authoritarianism, at least in the broader, ideological sense. Unfortunately, they may falter when applying this ideology at a more basic level, in their own groups. When actual difficulties arise within our own circles, many people want to find a quick exit route, some strategy for efficiently dealing with intractable or impossible people and situations. As soon as the collective trust fails, people tend to fall back into good old authoritarianism. When that starts to happen, the swing of the pendulum can be severe. Suddenly, a community based on reaching out to one another in solidarity can become a circus of Machiavellian maneuverings or outright collective viciousness. (We realize this may sound extreme, but it does happen, and it's not even all that rare.)

A group that pays lip service to egalitarianism but does not in its collective gut trust the basic principles of equality, democracy or consensus will reserve for itself a clause that allows it to avoid dwelling on such high principles during a difficult conflict. This clause usually involves suppressing disruptive behaviors or even expelling people.

In collectives that base their ideology on anarchist principles like autonomy and anti-authoritarianism

(whether they do this somewhat loosely or more specifically), the idea of expulsion is often justified by reference to the anarchist notion of "banning."

In a common anarchist vision of society, people would live or operate in groups with no leaders, making all community decisions by means of direct democracy. (In other words, everyone should be able to participate in such decisions and, ideally, consent to them.) If somebody somehow sabotages the community or otherwise causes or threatens serious harm, there are no police or other authoritarian forms of enforcement to handle the matter; therefore, the best way for the community to deal with the offender is to democratically banish her. This practice is believed to be less authoritarian than the conventional methods of criminal justice and attendant imprisonment, since the person is still free to seek out association with other communities. The crucial factor that is often overlooked by present-day collectives is that banning is meant to be reserved for extreme, dangerous, or criminal behavior, not as a way to get rid of someone whom some group members simply find unpleasant or inconvenient.

Out of curiosity, we searched classic anarchist texts looking for the origin of the concept of banning. While there are many references to voluntary association and the corollary notion of voluntary disassociation, they usually refer to the association (and the disassociation) of various groups. (And not to the all-too-common leap that "disassociation" simply means giving someone a swift kick in the pants, all the way out

the door.) We haven't found any explicit endorsement of expelling individuals for the good of the collective. The closest reference that we could find was in Malatesta's "A Talk about Anarchist-Communism," where he writes that the majority cannot be held hostage to the whims of the minority: "These malcontents cannot fairly demand that the wishes of many others should be sacrificed for their sakes." But the assumption here is that the minority, or an individual, could somehow force the group to accede to its wishes, and that's the scenario that concerns Malatesta. In today's activist groups, it's hard to imagine how one person could somehow make the group abide by her wishes.

And if someone is making unreasonable demands, wouldn't it be more humane simply to overrule her than to ban her? Or are we to conclude that overruling someone is not democratic but showing them the door is?

Bakunin writes that "vicious and parasitic individuals" who don't contribute to society with their labor can be stripped of their rights, but they have a choice to get those rights back "as soon as they begin to live by their own labor." This isn't an issue that is closely relevant to activist collectives, because members don't depend on the collective for survival. He also writes that those "who violate voluntary agreements, steal,

inflict bodily harm, or above all, violate the freedom of any individual, will be penalized according to the laws of society," but that they retain "the right to escape punishment by declaring that they wish to resign from that association." In both cases, individuals can choose not to be expelled if they agree to accept the group's sanctions, and in both examples, the case is being made for how to deal with serious criminal or antisocial behavior, not as a means to deal with a member of a community who is simply an annoyance.

We are not suggesting that the writings of Bakunin, Malatesta, or any other influential anarchist should be taken as gospel (so to speak!). Yet, when people talk about the right of expulsion as a built-in tenet in anarchism, they are implying that there is some justifying gospel, which does not exist.

Most of the time, the dreary scenario unfolds something like this: an all-around annoyance with a given person or situation has reached critical mass, and everybody is now steamed. The group is more than ready to take supposedly effective action against the supposed culprit. Soon enough, either the poor accused sap will flee, unable to tolerate the abuse that has ensued, or a ban will be called for, and it will probably succeed. If the ban does not succeed, the outcome

can be even messier: two factions will form, one in support of the ban and the other against it. Unless one side is strong enough to crush the other, the collective will break apart. Both outcomes are regrettable. At best, a human being has been vilified and humiliated. At worst, the group will have dissolved, amidst rancor, hurt feelings, and recriminations.

This unfortunate pattern can have irreparably painful and discouraging consequences for the accused or ostracized individual, dampening or eliminating a once enthusiastic desire to be involved in activism. In fact, the most disillusioned activists whom we have encountered did not become disillusioned for the typically cited reasons of state oppression, loss of basic ideals, or an increase in "adult" responsibility. Mostly, these activists got discouraged by the things that they saw and experienced within their own activist groups. The issues that their experiences bring up obviously extend far beyond personal injury suffered by isolated, "difficult" individuals. These problems actually raise fundamental questions about whether egalitarian collectives can be sustainable. Even when a collective survives such conflicts and ugliness, we're left wondering whether it survived with its principles and integrity intact.

RESPECT FOR DIFFERENCES

MANY COLLECTIVES ARE aware that they need to do better in addressing racism, sexism, homophobia, and other societal prejudices within their own ranks, but too many fail to address the reality that lack of respect for differences does not start with its ugliest and most glaring manifestations but is present whenever room is not made for another person's viewpoint, situation, or life experience.

The hand-wringing and self-blame that collectives engage in as an attempt to address their own internal problems with insensitivity are unlikely to yield useful results. Prejudice does not come in separate compartments. It's not okay to be against racism, sexism, and homophobia while being indifferent to the myriad other ways in which people are discriminatory toward one another or fail to understand one another's perspective or experience. If we want to be inclusive, it's not enough merely to identify particular historically oppressed groups whom we want to include and accept; we also need to be aware that differences come in a lot of varieties and packages. A dissimilarity as slight as an awkward social manner, imperfect language skills, or a reticent, or even obnoxious personality can be enough to cast someone as weird or tiresome, and her opinions therefore pre-judged as unimportant.

Tolerance begins with the acknowledgement that people other than ourselves may see things differently, and is shown when we suspend judgment while those with whom we may disagree or whose ideas we may not understand are given a forum to explain their perspective and are actively listened to. No one can presume to know how someone's life has shaped him or her. When the group makes such assumptions about someone, it is failing to respect differences.

Collectives that are built around a particular issue are often quite homogenous. Members would like to embrace differences, in theory, but when they're actually confronted with someone whose life is unlike theirs, they many find it difficult to see beyond their own limited experience. When we do poorly even at accepting personal differences and quirks, how can we expect to reach out to one another across broader differences that arise from race, ethnicity, class, sexual orientation, and gender?

In a collective that is, for example, made up primarily of young students or recent graduates, an older person with a day job and/or a family to take care of might be shut out of the group's work simply because most members of the collective didn't give a second thought to scheduling meetings late at night. Members' disabilities or health issues are also often unacknowledged by healthy people: it's not easy to put oneself in someone else's shoes and realize it may be hard for a person to attend regular planning for events or work long hours. When a member cannot contribute fully to a group's activities, he may be left out merely due to careless disregard for his difficulties: "Well, you weren't there so we decided to do it this way." Or, worse, groups may consciously and deliberately marginalize those who don't do as much work or are not present as often, without giving any consideration to the individuals' circumstances. Illness, family, work commitments, and financial situations are all differences that an egalitarian collective must attend to if it is truly to operate democratically.

Members of any group who don't have a computer are often rendered into nonentities because they cannot participate in email discussions. Many times no one even bothers to keep them apprised of events and meeting times. If you assume that everyone in a group should be able to afford a computer, that is completely at odds with the realities that social activism exists to address. Likewise, it is exclusionary to assume that even those who have computers will always be internet-savvy. A collective cannot function equitably when some of its members are systematically or carelessly excluded from its activities.

On a related matter...

It is reprehensible to use ugly social ills like racism and sexism as a pretext to assassinate the character of perceived enemies. When a fellow collective member has acted inappropriately, his particular actions should be addressed by the complainant, rather than jumping to broad character assassination. Calling him a sexist, even when it's arguably true, is unhelpful in resolving conflicts. Such charges are impossible to defend against: being sexist is too ugly to be excused (therefore no one can come to the person's defense without appearing to condone sexism) and too unspecific to be refuted.

Sometimes statements that no one would even think of considering as racist or sexist when said in isolation are read as such depending on the identity of the participants. A good example of this problem once occurred when a white male member of our collective was admonished at a coalition meeting for asking a woman of color to provide a more rational argument for the position that she was taking. He was told, subsequent to the debate, that his request for rational argument was both racist and sexist. The reason given was that white men throughout history have dismissed the opinions of women and people of color as not being sufficiently rational, and that rationality itself is a concept repeatedly used to reinforce patriarchy—which is, as a point of fact, demonstrably true. Yet in the situation that existed, this member of our collective was honestly unable to understand the other party's point and was making a good-faith effort to ask for clarification. The collective needs to ensure that people are able to ask questions and participate fully in discussions without having to face accusations of ignorance or insensitivity when they genuinely intend no offense.

An allegation of sexism or racism can also sometimes be used as a ploy to silence dialogue and force group censure or ostracism against an individual. If, instead, an offender is confronted with complaints about specific behaviors, the possibility exists that he will understand his mistakes and work to rectify them. After that hurdle has been crossed, it may well be appropriate to address broader issues.

It's important to recognize that within a relatively small group, which many collectives tend to be, unequal power dynamics are not usually limited to, nor at times even the result of, individuals' identification as members of either an oppressed or privileged societal group. A domineering versus a timid personality, a person's personal charisma or lack thereof, and whether or not one has allies or is well-liked within the group can play just as large a role in determining who has any power within the collective and can affect who will exercise the most influence and who will be marginalized or shut out.

PERSONAL VS. GROUP ISSUES

SOMETIMES, TWO PEOPLE caught up in a personal and emotional kind of war will insist on dragging the whole collective into their squabble, each (or sometimes only one) person demanding that the group censure the other.

The person who has greater power within the group, a stronger personality, or the ability to make the best case for being the most aggrieved might then very well succeed in gathering an indignant, angry mob to rally against the other party.

It is sometimes helpful for a small number of collective members, perhaps one to three, to intervene as intermediaries between the warring parties and help them find an appropriate means to resolve the conflict, at least to an extent that will allow them to continue functioning as collective members. For instance, it may be useful to find neutral mediators outside the group. But it is altogether inconsistent with the spirit of consensus and egalitarianism, which presupposes equal respect for each individual and his or her contribution to the group, for the collective to act as judge and jury (or bloodthirsty villagers carrying torches) in a situation that is emotionally painful for those involved and about which the collective cannot and should not know all the details.

Public conflict resolution, while certainly a better alternative than jumping to collective conclusions and decisions based on rumors and innuendo, puts the parties in the embarrassing position of having to explain private choices (of which they may not be particularly proud) in front of everybody. This tactic is likely only to lead to defensiveness, refusal to yield one's ground for fear of losing face, and further hurt feelings.

A collective may come up with the argument that internal disputes harm the image of the group to potential outside supporters and must therefore be suppressed by distancing one of the parties from its activities. Yet, this idea is highly authoritarian, and it is likely to do greater damage to the collective by breaking it apart rather than working to bring it together. Moreover, it leads to the logical conclusion that the best way to preserve harmony in the group is to simply not tolerate conflict.

A converse sort of problem also occurs fairly often: someone raises a legitimate grievance about the inappropriate way another member is conducting herself within the sphere of the collective's activities, then finds himself being accused of bringing the complaint up to the collective merely because of a personal dislike.

This instance involves an abuse of the collective process, usually by a self-appointed leader who does not wish to answer for her actions—who will therefore seek to distract from any criticism by claiming that the complainant has a personal problem rather than a legitimate concern. And soon, the poor soul who had the audacity to call the leader to task might find himself slandered, vilified, or attacked with verbal invectives meant to frighten him into submission.

At this point, some well-meaning collective members might respond to all the interpersonal tension by urging everyone to chill. They might even spout a bunch of well-meaning platitudes such as, "What's important is the group's work" (which should not be sidelined by "petty bickering," of course). And to uninformed passersby, this might seem like a good assessment, a reasonable answer given in the interest of peace. In truth, however, such a reaction is simply callous and insensitive. It's symptomatic of the kind of thoughtlessness that results when gullible people allow their leader to manipulate them. (Although, that's not to say that it can't also sometimes be used as a deliberate tactic as well....)

We believe that in this kind of situation, the collective must simply encourage the dissenter to speak up. The group should not allow a dissenting opinion to be stifled simply so that they can avoid further conflict. That is a false kind of peace, a perpetuation of injustice that does not suit a group that's (supposedly) seeking to create a more democratic society.

MICRO-MANAGING OTHER PEOPLE'S BEHAVIOR

IN A WELL-INTENTIONED attempt to establish guidelines to prevent disrespect of one another and abuse of process, some collectives fall into the authoritarian trap of dictating which specific, often minute, behaviors collective members may or may not display. Those who do not strictly adhere to the regulations, perhaps even unwittingly, may be frowned upon, smarmily chastised, or rendered into undesirables.

Self-appointed leaders who are adept at working the group's process can use strict adherence to nit-picking rules as a way to put themselves up as role models (since they always follow the letter, though not the spirit, of the rules). Then, they can paint those who may not be so versed in the minutia of the guidelines, or so slick about appearing to follow them, as saboteurs. The hapless or gauche, who might commit blunders like using inappropriate terminology or speaking out of turn, thus become easy victims for the "process tyrants."

Behavioral guidelines cannot substitute for basic respect, decency, common sense, or an honest attempt to listen, understand, and strive for fairness. Any attempt to narrowly codify and restrict normal human interactions and ordinary faux-pas can create a tightly wound atmosphere of coercion and disapproval.

Interrupting

A lot has been made in activist circles about the inappropriateness of interrupting someone when he or she is talking. Interrupting is almost always obnoxious and can be used, sometimes intentionally, to dominate, but it is also a common human fallacy. Some people are chronic interrupters: they may be so brimming with exciting ideas or information that they just can't contain themselves. Such individuals can usually be handled with joking, light-handed rebukes or by simply interrupting them in return. Others are long-winded droners. While everyone should be given their space to speak, it's not necessarily wrong to gently interrupt those who have been boring the collective with endless, repetitive speeches. They should not be silenced, of course, but they can be made aware of the effects of their verbosity.

Not everybody has the same skill at navigating interpersonal exchanges. Some people are not good at recognizing that split second when someone has finished talking and it's okay to jump in. They are the ones who are most likely to interrupt, and be reprimanded for it, while they also, ironically, are the least likely to get a word out and have their opinions heard.

While facilitation and hand-raising should prevent this, there will always be circumstances when people are engaging in informal conversations, whether in or out of meetings.

It's also fairly normal, in everyday speech, to interrupt someone to nip a misunderstanding in the bud: "Oh, no, no. I'm sorry I made it sound that way. What I meant was…." Collective process needs to take ordinary interaction into account. We should not try to dictate actions that are awkward and artificial and then frown on people who don't immediately take to them.

Stacking

Prohibiting any and all interruptions can become a problem at meetings when added to the strict stipulation that members can only speak in the order in which they raise their hands. Hand-raising is a good idea, since it stops people from merely shouting over each other to be heard, as is making a list, or stack, that determines whose fair turn it is to talk. Yet, these practices, if applied too rigidly, can easily stifle discussion or facilitate abuses.

For instance, someone may intentionally make untrue and damaging statements about a proposed project in an attempt to denigrate it. The person who made the original proposal may be desperate to say something, but he can't because he mustn't interrupt, and there are others in line to speak. If the proposal maker speaks up out of order he will, in all likelihood, be looked at with opprobrium, only adding to the denigrator's case that his project is suspect. If he waits until it's his rightful turn to talk, it may be too late to undo other members' already-solidifying inaccurate perceptions. It makes no sense to use hand-raising merely to make a list without allowing for the fact that discussions require an exchange. When questions go unanswered or falsehoods unchallenged, there can be no discourse.

What often happens is that someone will raise his hand to respond to something that has just been said; by the time it's his turn to speak, there may have been another ten comments made on other matters, and what the person had raised his hand to say is no longer on point. Since it will be his only chance to talk, however, he will still take his turn. Multiply this by the number of people in the meeting, and you have a random list of utterances and no semblance of a discussion or healthy debate.

The door is opened to speech-making by the self-important while the meek or shy may only get a few words out and not receive another opportunity to explain themselves more fully.

There has to be some way for people to be allowed to clarify points when necessary without exposing themselves to outraged censure.

Prioritizing

Many collectives have made rules that require facilitators to give priority to members of traditionally oppressed groups. While the intention is commendable, in practice it's not an easy task to determine which individuals in a particular group are more or less likely to be overlooked or silenced. Power inequities within a small group of people can stem from a great many factors that are not easily reduced, for example, to race or gender. Thus, anyone who attempts to combat injustice by applying overly broad criteria might actually perpetuate even more injustice.

It is important to make sure that those who have been quiet get a chance to be heard. But, once again, the rule must not be applied in the absence of common sense. Anyone should feel free to say, "I have no comment." In addition, people who are directly involved in a given issue, or are themselves raising a matter for the group to consider, are likely to have more to say when it comes up for discussion and may even be questioned by the group to elucidate and clarify relevant points. They should not be silenced because someone else has not said as much on the topic. It makes no sense for someone who brings up a concern to be prohibited from participating in the ensuing discussion simply because he or she has used up the allotted speaking time.

SKEPTICISM IS HEALTHY

BEING SKEPTICAL IS not the same as being distrustful or suspicious, both of which can undermine a collective's honest interactions, as well as play tricks with one's own judgment. It simply means not jumping to conclusions, neither positive nor negative, before having investigated an issue.

Coming to a hasty, negative opinion of another person, as many of us know, is often ugly and can turn out to be grossly unfair. Furthermore, since most of us don't like to admit it when we're wrong, the bad reputation can actually persist even after the facts have proven the condemnation to be unwarranted. But a thoughtless positive judgment can be damaging too. We might give somebody's words too much importance, because she gives the impression of being exceptionally knowledgeable or effective, for instance, and unwittingly follow unwise advice or even turn over control of the group (always a bad idea).

Some of the most despicable injustices that happen in collectives are perpetrated by those of us who were only trying to help. A fellow collective member comes up to you, clearly upset and outraged, and tells you about someone who's been making his or her life hell. As a good friend, your reaction is probably to sympathize, listen, and ask what you can do. You may even take it upon yourself to alert others of the problem. Thus, the wheels of a rumor, or worse, a baseless character assassination, have just been set in motion. By you.

We are not suggesting that you be stingy with your sympathy and emotional support, only that you keep in mind that every story has two sides, and that it's usually not prudent to act until the matter has been explored a little more thoroughly. In many cases, whenever two sides of a story are clearly divergent and emotions are running high, it's best to begin a formal grievance or conflict resolution proceeding.

It's not uncommon for members who feel they have been aggrieved in some way to circulate a petition, asking other members to sign off on some kind of sanction against the presumed transgressor, whether it's a temporary ban or a demand they seek counseling. In our experience, people are generally all too happy, in an effort to be supportive and mindful of the best interests of the group, to sign on to an accusation about which they have absolutely no first-hand knowledge, sometimes even excoriating a person they have never met. Needless to say, this is not a sign of healthy group dynamics. Even if the people jumping on the bandwagon are well-meaning, they are abdicating their responsibilities to the collective by acting without having done their homework. And those circulating the grievance may feel they have been genuinely wronged, but they are circumventing group process when they bypass due process and an open forum for the airing of complaints. Unfortunately, we have also seen instances in which getting rid of someone is an intentional, calculated act, where the group is manipulated into believing it is acting in the collective best interest by participating in an undemocratic ostracism.

Ironically, a converse kind of phenomenon is also not uncommon, where a member who has had to tolerate victimization and abuse by someone in the group seeks help from the collective and is roundly ignored. Personal power politics tend to come into play in these cases: an unpopular or not highly regarded person who complains about someone who is seen as a leader or a more valued member may find himself alone and a target for ridicule. The proper way for the group to proceed in either circumstance (whether they believe the accused or the accuser) is to investigate the situation, call for formal procedures, such as previously agreed-upon conflict resolution protocols, and allow all parties to air their concerns. Regardless of who you believe to be right or wrong—whether it's the defendant or the complainant—making hasty judgments never serves the interests of fairness. Neither does calling for sanctions (such as ad hoc banning, the popular favorite) which are excessive or unnecessary for resolving a given circumstance.

It may not be possible to know exactly what the truth is in a particular situation, but one can come to an educated judgment based on ascertainable facts and the probable likelihood of certain events having taken place rather than others, for instance by considering the motivation that someone might have to dissemble or stretch the truth.

VAGUENESS LEADS TO AUTHORITARIANISM

OFTEN, THERE IS not enough clarity among members of egalitarian collectives regarding how egalitarianism is supposed to work. Because the individuals involved do not know exactly what to do, there is inaction and frustration, leaving the door wide open for someone or some small cabal to rush in like a knight in shining armor and rescue the collective by taking charge.

A number of people with whom we've spoken about the difficulties of working collectively are not concerned with power inequities, which they do not see as a particular problem of their own group, but with slow meetings and fruitless discussions of trivialities; not knowing who is supposed to do what or how to delegate functions; and either things not getting done or only one or two people doing all the work.

People get tired of waiting around for every issue to come out into the open and get thoroughly discussed at meetings. Sometimes the meetings aren't even held, or the people who have an interest in the particular matter don't show up, or not enough people show up, which means the discussion has to be postponed once again. Sometimes it simply seems easier to allow decisions to be made by a few, even without asking the rest of the group. At least that way things get done. These common problems, however, create a fertile ground for an authoritarian to take over, to bring order and function to the group—often to everyone's relief and gratitude.

When that happens, there has been a serious breakdown of basic egalitarian principles. There may be one of two dynamics underlying this phenomenon (or, possibly, both occurring at once and reinforcing each other): either someone is manipulating the group to grab power for himself or his little clique (which he might even be doing unconsciously—some people just have bossiness and leadership in their blood); or many (maybe all) of the group's members are afraid to take responsibility for making decisions and doing the work that is needed to move the group forward. When everyone waits for someone else to decide what to do, nothing happens. The result is recriminations and mutual resentment, which can destroy a group. In egalitarian collectives, there are no leaders to light a fire under everyone's collective butt: everyone has to be his and her own motivator, initiator and carry-through-ator.

Common Misunderstandings of Consensus

The most fundamental misunderstanding of consensus is that everybody has to agree. There is often a lot of pressure not to express any disagreements or reservations so as not to appear uncooperative. Proposals pass simply because no one dares to raise an objection. That is not consensus. What should happen, in a nutshell, is that someone makes a proposal, people ask for explanation and clarification, the merits of the proposal are discussed, and maybe small amendments are made as the discussion proceeds. The final version of the proposal is brought to a vote. (Yes, you still vote in consensus. The difference from processes that we normally call voting is that in consensus, the group has to vote for something unanimously in order for it to pass. We find that actually taking the time to vote makes it clear what people's wishes are, rather than assuming consent if all just keep silent.) If everyone agrees to the proposal as is, it passes. If someone has objections or reservations, the proposal needs to be amended in such a way that it will meet the concerns raised. The crucial element is to ask the person objecting to explain what she objects to so that the group can find a solution for which everyone will give their consent.

Many groups fall into a quagmire of disorganization because they feel that creating a structure for getting things done is somehow authoritarian, especially if it is accomplished primarily by one person. Not so. As long as all actions are transparent and everyone is given a chance to question them, to voice their concerns and see them addressed, and as long as decisions are put to a vote by which everyone consents to them, initiatives that are the brainchild of one person are perfectly acceptable. It's okay for someone who has a knack for keeping things in order to create a schedule, for instance, or a file of useful addresses, as long as she brings it to the group for approval. The thing to look out for is covert intimidation, e.g., if someone acts all hurt if everybody does not show unmitigated appreciation for her efforts by rubber-stamping whatever she wants to do. And a lack of transparency is also a major red flag: any information that anyone has put together must always be available to the entire collective, and any action a member undertakes on the collective's behalf must be with the collective's knowledge and approval.

On the other hand, when there are small decisions to be made that do not relate to fundamental principles, it's perfectly OK to delegate them to an appropriate committee. For instance, if a planning committee receives general approval from the collective on how much to spend for an event, that committee does not have to get a vote from the whole collective on every type of supply it wishes to order. Nonetheless, it does have to present a list of expenditures and revenues after the fact.

Skill Sharing

Another reason things sometimes get bogged down in inactivity is inadequate skill sharing. Tasks like organizing an event, planning the group's activities, figuring out how to pay for things, and doing outreach all require skills that should be learned by working with someone who already has some experience. "Skills" are not just manual abilities like sewing, woodworking, or cooking. Organizational, technological, and interpersonal skills also must be shared and learned.

Sometimes collectives assume that because everyone in the group is equal, everyone can be counted on to autonomously take over any and all tasks without any prior knowledge and without any assistance. There is often a misconception of what "autonomy" and "DIY" stand for, which can lead to the belief that everyone should be able to work independently, without ever asking for advice from someone more knowledgeable or experienced. The whole idea that some people may be more experienced than others is looked on as suspect. Indeed, even offering guidance may be seen as paternalistic and hierarchical. That point of view is healthy in some respects, since no one should be looked at as being somehow more important, nor should anyone's opinions carry more weight, but it is self defeating when it leads to denying or ignoring reality. It doesn't make sense for members with no experience to be left on their own to take on responsibilities that are completely new to them. The result is general frustration among members because things are not getting done or getting done poorly, feelings of anxiety and guilt among individuals for having rashly volunteered to take on a project that one is not actually able to bring to fruition, and the all-too-common result that the usual suspects take over and save the day. Or the group's hopeful efforts get lost in mediocrity and ineffectualness.

Clarity is the antidote to muddling through. If a group spells out as clearly as possible how things will be accomplished and how the necessary skills will be passed down, it will avoid problems that could eventually lead to power struggles in the collective. We have actually seen groups in which the more senior members scoffed at the idea of training newer members, claiming they had no time to waste on babysitting. That is a blazing red flag that not even the most basic notion of egalitarianism is operating in the group!

IS THIS THE JUST SOCIETY WE WANT TO MODEL?

A MODEL FOR JUSTICE?

COLLECTIVES WHO CHOOSE to base their organizational structure on equality, direct democracy, and/or consensus usually do so, at least in part, to model the just society we would like to see in the world at large. Social change involves not only campaigning for radical reform in the broader society but also being, or embodying, the better world we hope to bring about through activism. This fundamental belief can and should be used by egalitarian collectives to inform the decisions and actions they take, especially when it comes to how group members treat one another.

It doesn't make any sense for an activist organization to be fighting for justice and social equality while at the same time allowing back-stabbing, nasty rumors, and manipulative power plays to dominate or influence the internal interactions of the group. Yet, this happens all the time. At times it's intentional: one or a few members control the group by creating feuds and distrust; the persons or positions they favor prevail while those they wish to eliminate are made to seem suspect and fall by the wayside. Other times injustice is the result of bungling ineptitude or lack of clarity or knowledge about how egalitarian systems can be expected to work.

Often, an organization insists on using consensus, which in many activist scenes is treated as the only acceptable form of decision making for any group that wants to call itself radical—to the point of faddishness—without any real understanding of how consensus functions and what it can and cannot accomplish. People may expect that cooperation and mutual understanding will automatically flow out of the consensus process. As a result, the group creates no guidelines for dealing with friction or other interpersonal difficulties. They may even feel that rules are antithetical to personal autonomy. Autonomy is itself interpreted as being synonymous with selfishness, therefore selfishness is considered well and good.

When the inevitable conflicts crop up, the radical egalitarian collective often does not even have in place the conventional forms of fair dealing that are built into mainstream society, such as the judicial process. Instead, in handling (real or perceived) offenders, collective members tend to skip right over any notions of due process, since they don't think an egalitarian group should have any need for all that bureaucratic baggage, and proceed straight to the basest of human instincts: name-calling, spreading or repeating baseless allegations, lying to cover up one's own bad behavior, and—everyone's favorite— banning, usually perpetrated out of hand and in anger, without anyone looking into any of the alleged facts nor allowing the accused to offer any defense.

We need to ask ourselves: is this the just society that we want to model? Wholesale expulsion from an activist group is painful enough, but when that happens one can still go on with the rest of one's life. What if the group in question were the community where one lives, works and has familial ties? Would we want to be a part of a world where a person can be expelled from his community because others find him annoying or inconvenient, or because he loses his temper, and where people can malign, slander, and judge him without even his having a fundamental right to a forum where he can speak up for himself?

Many of us rightly condemn the injustices of the societies in which we live, but then we fail to turn that same scrutiny and skepticism onto our own activist organizations and anti-authoritarian collectives. Do we accord one another at least the rights that are written into the United States' system of justice? (The authors live in the U.S.) Or are we even more authoritarian and less just than mainstream institutions whenever we condone the wholesale condemnation of people and behaviors we may not even know firsthand, and when we fail to establish fair procedures to air grievances and resolve conflicts?

THE DEARTH OF DUE PROCESS

Due Process of law implies the right of the person affected thereby to be present before the tribunal which pronounces judgment upon the question of life, liberty, or property, in its most comprehensive sense; to be heard, by testimony or otherwise, and to have the right of controverting, by proof, every material fact which bears on the question of right in the matter involved. If any question of fact or liability be conclusively presumed against him, this is not due process of law.

—*Black's Law Dictionary*, 6th Edition, page 500

In other chapters, we discussed some of the aspects of collective process that pertain to fair decision making within egalitarian groups. However, these different issues might have varying degrees of importance in relation to the broader notion of how a fair and democratic society should function. And in that sense, due process is essential.

Among the definitions of due process, the item above, from *Black's Law Dictionary*, will suffice as well as any. The basic concept of due process is that no one should be assumed to have committed any violation without having a fair hearing in front of people who can judge her impartially according to reasonable objective standards and without prejudice. Essential to the fairness of such a hearing is the idea that anyone accused has the right to face her accusers and defend herself (or have an expert defend her, if the complexity of the laws or process require it). Stated simply, everyone is innocent until proven guilty by just and fair means.

This idea is very well established in mainstream culture and society. In fact, it has been established in all concepts of modern democracy ever since modern democracy developed, during the Middle Ages. It can be traced back to English common law and the Magna Carta. This is why a basic text such as *Black's Law Dictionary* (a very mainstream text found in any stuffy law firm) contains such a good, concise and fair definition of the term. It is also why there are significant references to due process in two Amendments to the U.S. Constitution (Fifth and Fourteenth). While the legal systems and agents of the State may do things to undermine due process, and the police and courts sometimes blatantly violate it, the concept itself is considered legitimate in all corners of legal argument. It is not, by any means, radical or utopian.

Unfortunately, once we look at the conduct of many egalitarian collectives, due process does begin to look like a radical idea. This is a disturbing irony. Egalitarian collectives are supposed to build upon the basic concepts of democracy and strive to make things more democratic. The people within these collectives are supposed to view the basic standards of fairness in conventional society as being relatively minimal compared to those of the society that we all want to build. And yet, sadly, as we examine the process (or lack thereof) among many of our egalitarian comrades, such standards often seem to comprise a maximal, nearly unattainable goal.

In a number of cases, we have witnessed the following sort of process take place after someone has been accused:

The accused may be told about problems that people are having with something he did, but specifics are rarely mentioned, and a fair hearing is never suggested. Bad words and rumors are accumulated against the accused, often in forums that he cannot access, such as hidden meetings or special e-mail lists. A closed-door meeting takes place in which it is decided that the accused has caused certain problems or committed certain violations or crimes. Evidence is said to have been produced, but the accused never knows what that evidence, exactly, was. A judgment is made in the accused's absence, and the poor accused individual becomes the last person to know about the conviction and the sentence (which usually involves some deprivation of liberty—such as ending that person's participation in a given group). In sum, there is no fair hearing, no right of self-defense by the accused against the accusers, and no adequate revelation of the charges or reasons provided for the penalties. Some sort of trial takes place in which everything is wrong.

We would be outraged if this happened even within a single collective, but we have found that this awful mockery of justice occurs dismayingly often.

There may be a number of reasons why collectives are experiencing this dearth of due process. The most common may be that people who call themselves "anarchists" or "anti-authoritarians" are used to rebelling against rules, and many will use their opposition to authority as an excuse to reject any and all rules at their convenience.

A lot of people might get this idea about "anarchism" from rebellious subcultures that have a very individualistic and possibly nihilistic focus. For instance, in the past few decades (and then some), many people in radical groups spent some formative time in the punk rock movement(s). Certainly, punk has been a positive influence sometimes: it has fostered egalitarian attitudes, starting with the democratization of performance (i.e., by encouraging the idea that anyone in the crowd can become one of the artists and rejecting the passive star worship that has often characterized mainstream rock). There is nothing wrong with coming into a collective with that kind of attitude; it is very appropriate. On the other hand, a collective will probably not be helped by those people (punks and lots of others) who think that freedom simply means rejecting all ideas as well as all rules.

A true authoritarian might benefit greatly from some rebels' instinct to reject all rules, since that also means rejecting rules that have been developed to check the power of authoritarians. And that category definitely includes the rules of due process.

Contrary to the sloppy thinking that is all too common, there is no situation in which someone has been accused of something serious (i.e., a deed that might warrant limitation of freedoms or exclusion entirely) that can be addressed fairly while ignoring due process. Moreover, due process is not, contrary to what some might think, merely a way that a society deals with the commission of crimes. One of the main reasons for due process is that we often don't even know, until there has been a fair and impartial proceeding, whether a crime or transgression has been committed. Even more often, even when we know that someone has done something that upset people, we can't be sure about the nature, degree, or seriousness of her actions—at least not until they can be investigated in a fair and impartial way.

Without due process, not only do we risk the unfair treatment of known criminals and a poorly planned way of dealing with crime; we also run the risk that crimes might be completely invented and people might be turned into criminals for reasons

that have nothing to do with anything that actually happened. Without due process, anybody runs the risk of being made a criminal by individuals or cliques who hold power, who feel in any way challenged or threatened by the accused. Without due process, even people who do not have any power or influence might easily vilify someone who is innocent if they can figure out how to influence or manipulate a powerful individual or clique. Due process, followed correctly, is the specific mechanism through which innocent dissenters and iconoclasts can often make sure that they are not instantly, unjustly turned into villains or pariahs.

Sometimes, people feel that due process should be altered or circumvented when the person(s) making the accusations belong to a traditionally oppressed group. This is a problematic concept that is actually supported by many people on the left. For instance, an accusation of racism or sexism stemming from an argument might be acted upon without adequate investigation of the contents of the disagreement or the intentions of the accused. Intentions are sometimes simply assumed, without anyone asking for proof. Often, out of some eagerness to pursue an "anti-oppressive" policy, an egalitarian collective will approach an accusation with strong prejudice against the accused. At best, the burden of proof then falls upon the accused (i.e., he is guilty until proven innocent). At worst, there is no proof even requested: the accusation itself is considered sufficient.

Take another look at the last sentence of the excellent definition of due process above: "If any question of fact or liability be conclusively presumed against him, this is not due process of law." In the world of left-leaning or egalitarian groups and collectives, where people might have particularly strong desires to right certain wrongs found within our society, that is a thought well worth keeping in mind. Prejudice in judgment is unacceptable regardless of the gender, race, ethnic identity, or any personal characteristic of the accuser or the accused.

The presumption of guilt, in general, is an even more common problem than the blatant violation of due process that we described earlier. As we discussed in "Creating Pariahs," there are numerous ways that accusers and their allies can spread ill opinion long before a supposedly fair and just trial takes place. It is a frequent tactic of vilifiers to spread the bad word in forums to which the accused does not have access. As we have said before, when this tactic is used in advance of any trial, then the trial might as well not happen.

In standard legal practice here in the U.S., the accused theoretically has the right to change the place of trial when the immediate surroundings have already been poisoned with news or publicity that create prejudice. True, this usually happens when the accused is wealthy or famous or is being accused of an infamous crime, but this is a right that seems to be universally recognized, at least in principle. Unfortunately, within many egalitarian collectives, such a right seems not to be known at all. Thus, in circles within which someone has been totally vilified, and people have discussed and built up rumors to which the accused might not even have had access, the local "fair trial" is pursued anyway, as though it still could be fair.

This kind of situation is unacceptable in a collective committed to egalitarianism and fairness. When local rumors and accusations spread like wildfire, it is important to move the trial beyond the places where the fire has spread. That is why the local group from which a case originated is usually the last place where that case should be tried. If there is another place within the larger organization where a controversial or much-talked-about case might be moved, then it should be moved as soon as possible. If there is no group outside of the small local group involved, then maybe outside mediators should be called in.

There may be many more examples of the violation of due process within collectives. Nonetheless, we recommend that collectives address the most obvious and immediate problems, at least as a start. Egalitarian collectives owe it to themselves and others to pursue important principles such as due process in more advanced ways than conventional society, rather than acting as though they are ignorant of the conventions of justice that most people already recognize.

Admittedly, due process isn't in such great shape in mainstream society either. In the age of the PATRIOT Act, secret military tribunals, and the "War on Terror," the conventional rights that everyone knows about have been repeatedly trampled on or ignored. Many egalitarian groups, among other factions (both left and right), are fighting the good fight to protect people's civil liberties. However, groups may lose credibility if they don't protect the civil liberties within their own situations as well.

It is also important for people within egalitarian collectives to know what they're fighting for. By addressing the dearth of due process in their own circles and communities, these activists may also become more skilled and articulate in advocating for the new world that they would like to create. If they lose track of the basic principles of due process at the same time that due process is being stifled in the mainstream community, then the outcome might not be so good. The dearth of due process within our collectives might simply contribute to the death of due process everywhere.

WHAT ABOUT FREE SPEECH?

EVERYONE WHO SEEKS a more democratic society would naturally agree that freedom of speech is essential. Moreover, no egalitarian collective would ever claim to oppose freedom of speech. Yet, in practice, not all collectives (nor lefty groups in general) support free speech, whether it means allowing free speech in debate or on e-mail lists, or allowing other groups the same freedom to express themselves and demonstrate their own beliefs freely.

Regarding Free Speech at Meetings

In order to allow freedom of speech at meetings, groups need to create an atmosphere in which all the participants feel maximally comfortable about expressing themselves. If any people feel at any time that their ways of self-expression, their choice of words, or their tone or approach simply can't meet a group's particular standards, then they certainly will not have a chance to enjoy the true freedom to speak or participate.

This is true whenever the homogeneity of a group might be seen by an interested observer as intimidating or unwelcoming. Many of us are aware that more effort should be made in activist circles to include diverse viewpoints, yet we overlook some simple steps we could take to be more inclusive and approachable, such as easing up on demanding that people adhere to the most stringently correct jargon. Whenever we raise a collective eyebrow at someone who says "reform" instead of "shut down" or "vote" instead of "reach consensus," we are stifling dialogue.

Now, of course, there are limits in terms of propriety. It is understood that people shouldn't be espousing views that are way off the mark in terms of the focus of the collective—e.g., in most collectives, it would not be appropriate to launch into a completely right-wing kind of agenda. However, this problem occurs extremely rarely, and when it does occur, the instigator is usually simply ignored. More often, at a meeting, people whose opinions are perfectly relevant will feel overly inhibited or cautious regarding how they express those opinions. Too often, for example, members of a collective feel pressured to watch every word they speak for fear that they might unknowingly and unintentionally reveal some connotations of racism or sexism. Unfortunately, this strict kind of political correctness often helps to ensure that the group's true reach remains limited to an extremely narrow range of people, i.e., those who are well-trained regarding what terms, phrases, or methods of speaking are politically fashionable and acceptable.

We are not saying that people should be encouraged to babble sexist or racist slurs—and if they do, certainly other members of a group have the right to protest freely. Yet, self-conscious political correctness within these groups has sometimes gotten extreme enough that some participants—especially among those who are not part of an acknowledged oppressed identity group—are double-checking every word they say. We think it's a shame that people feel a need to be this self-conscious.

At the same time, the patterns that have allowed the bossy and outspoken to dominate agendas persist. Each of us carries his or her own baggage into group discussions culled from a lifetime of experience: the sense of entitlement that is wrought by a privileged upbringing; the self-congratulation that comes from years of praise and approbation; the sense of hopelessness that can come about from experiencing bad jobs and poverty; the self-doubt brought about by years of having been dismissed or criticized. Group members' feelings of either inadequacy or grandeur are not erased by an insistence on proper terminology.

It would be a shame if a large number of people in our community even occasionally resisted expressing their opinions simply because they felt that their comments might seem politically incorrect due to the race, gender, or ethnicity of the people involved in the debate. Likewise, those who aren't versed in the rhetoric of activism should not be made to feel that if they speak up they will be chastised on their choice of words. It is bad enough to feel overcautious about the content of one's arguments, but it is simply stifling to know that such content will also be heavily judged according to context. That situation would certainly not be conducive to free speech; in fact, it might result in an atmosphere that diminishes free expression for everyone, regardless of race, ethnicity, or gender.

Regarding Free Speech on the Internet

Within the radical activist community, there has lately been a frenzy to establish strict guidelines for e-mail lists, internet forums, and public comments on articles and blog postings, and to purge people whose comments on those venues are considered provocative or upsetting. This is a relatively recent phenomenon, as e-mail used to be a very free medium, back in the earlier days of the Internet.

Too often, we have seen e-mail lists, internet forums, and other interactive websites flooded with ideas about strict protocol to limit the things that are said. Very often, there are rules against "flaming," meaning that no one should say something that might be interpreted as a direct insult or attack on another person. While it is understandable that we don't want people to be scared away from lists and discussions by nasty or vicious infighting, we also think that honest conflict is essential to open debate. Moreover, it always becomes quite apparent that anti-flaming rules, by nature, are extremely subjective, and that the decision to ban or restrict list participation is usually made single-handedly by the website administrator or the supporting clique in power.

As with all the kinds of purges that we discussed in "Creating Pariahs," the people who are usually kicked off e-mail lists or interactive websites present no threat to the group and hold no power. They are often banned or restricted because people who do have power consider them to be annoying and/or disruptive. Yet the people who are kicked off these venues are rarely the true disrupters. While we often hear about how e-mail lists and activist websites need to guard against provocateurs and saboteurs, the people who deliberately provoke to undermine a group's politics are usually sufficiently shouted down and leave soon enough anyway.

Often, there are urgent pleas to silence or ban disruptive posters on the grounds that the group's work needs to be protected and given priority. Yet the work could very well continue unimpeded if people were willing simply to disregard postings they found offensive or personally disruptive instead of engaging and encouraging them. We have found that after an annoying subscriber is removed from an e-mail list, the traffic on that list often ceases, since there is no longer any provocation to get heated about. We believe that someone should be banned from a list, forum, or website only as an absolute last resort. (Perhaps only if the volume of mail or comments submitted by that one person is untenable—say, dozens of e-mails or comments every day....)

Meanwhile, we can't help noticing that those who do have power and influence with groups are rarely watched or criticized for any of their own aggressive Internet behavior, even as they drive to get others silenced or expelled. In other words, the people who are most eager to silence others are often simply the kind who can dish it out but can't take it. If too many such people are allowed to have their way, then the freedom that was once so prevalent in internet discussions will probably be lost forever.

Regarding Free Speech for Others

Just as we need to allow maximal freedom of speech within our own circles, we need to extend this principle outside of our circles, even if it means allowing the expression of views that horrify or disgust us. Otherwise, we will not truly be sticking to our own principles, we will lose moral credibility, and we might even leave ourselves open to charges of hypocrisy.

Ironically, some of the people on the left who make the most noise about not being allowed to speak or assemble freely are the same ones who might violently try to stop ideological opponents from exercising those freedoms.

Regarding Free Speech in Publications

Publications—such as newspapers and magazines—are a more complicated issue, because of limited space and editorial prerogative. Clearly, a publication devoted to a certain kind of viewpoint has a right to reject articles that are completely inappropriate, especially when space is limited. Nonetheless, a publication should at least stick to its own professed values. If a publication professes openness to a wide range of left-radical or anarchist viewpoints, then it shouldn't suddenly turn around and suppress some viewpoints for fear that they might be too controversial. If a publication has a letters or feedback section that is supposed to be open, then the editors shouldn't be cautiously screening those who disagree with them.

Freedom of speech becomes a bigger issue at a publication when the editors follow inconsistent or sloppy process. A publication that is supposed to be run or edited by a collective should stick to this principle. Unfortunately, some publications that claim to be run collectively really do have an editorial hierarchy with some chief editor to whom almost everyone defers, and that chief editor often is the ultimate judge of content. When that sort of hierarchy occurs, there is more danger that collective members may find their viewpoints suppressed.

One important guideline to keep in mind with regard to all editorial work is whether the editing done is actually necessary and/or helps to make the writing stronger, or whether the piece is chopped up more arbitrarily, for reasons having little to do with the strength of the writing. If the piece is edited in such a way as to cut out certain opinions being expressed, then we might begin to ask questions regarding freedom of expression. If the writer of the piece consistently finds that her articles are being chopped up more severely than others' even though the quality of her original writing might be at least as good as anyone else's (or perhaps even better), then it becomes clear that she is being subject to some arbitrary standards: are some editors who have more influence and power suppressing her writing because of their general opinions regarding her or her viewpoints? That sort of question certainly will raise issues regarding freedom of speech.

In General

We admit that freedom of speech or expression is not always a one hundred percent clear issue, especially when it must be weighed against seemingly contradictory principles such as editorial prerogative or the right of any given group or individual not to be treated disrespectfully. Nonetheless, in most cases, the choices are quite clear. Distasteful speech needs to be addressed with dialogue and engagement, in the spirit of increasing awareness and understanding on both sides. There are many ways in which groups that theoretically support freedom of speech need to be more careful about following their own stated principles. Almost always, if this kind of question even arises, it is best to err on the side of maximal freedom.

CRUELTY

IN A GROUP that is committed to equality and justice, the way that we choose to treat each other is vitally connected to what we hope to accomplish as activists. If we hope to bring about a fairer, more compassionate world, we have to start with our most basic interactions. The fact that deliberate cruelty does not lead to greater justice should be too obvious to mention. Yet in collectives it's very often considered normal, not even worthy of a mention or of a raised eyebrow. It's common practice to torment someone mercilessly until he flees the collective—or even the entire local activist scene—because he is so afraid of encountering further abuse. We've rarely heard anyone speak up to say that it's morally repugnant or to try to stop it in any way.

When people start to condone and accept cruelty as though it were simply business-as-usual, that can become a way of life. Such an approach will only promote social injustice and a more vicious, less tolerant world. Therefore, we must vigorously oppose cruelty whenever we find it within our own midst.

Too often, our activist collectives display the same kind of behavior that we saw as children in school playgrounds, where an individual was singled out for no other reason than that she was an easy mark. We can't help recalling such bad memories when a member of a collective is gleefully subjected to a campaign of abuse. Are we so conditioned by our upbringing in a society that forces us to conform to authority that whenever the mantle of established authority is removed (as it is in an egalitarian collective and in a playground), we can think of nothing better to do than prey on each other with cruel name-calling and senseless attacks? A frequent consequence of new-found freedom is to immediately establish and follow new hierarchies based on who is more popular or stronger, or the best at manipulation, versus who is unpopular, out of the group's mainstream, the easy target, etc. It's just like *Lord of the Flies*....

Individuals who believe they have been mistreated by their fellow group members feel genuine pain. Sometimes it can even have a profound effect on their lives. It is not possible or appropriate, in our view, to explain away somebody's pain by pointing to the group's positive work or invoking regulations that the pariah in question may or may not have properly followed. Do you honestly believe that anyone deserves to have cruelty visited upon her? Even if she's a pain in the ass, if she's impossible to deal with—even if she herself is cruel—that is no reason to taunt, torment, bully, slander with vicious lies, etc. As activists, we hope to create a world in which difficulties can be addressed and every attempt is made to resolve them, not one where suppression, intimidation, and violence (psychological or physical) are resorted to if the group's majority or most vocal members do not get their way.

It is not possible, in our view, for a person who feels pushed out or abused to simply be mistaken in perceiving a sustained campaign of attacks and vilification by the group (or a faction of the group). Even if an ugly situation can be explained away as a misunderstanding, it isn't possible for the victim to have misunderstood his own pain. The hurt that is expressed over and over in situation after situation is undoubtedly real, and it should not be dismissed, regardless of whether or not the person experiencing it was originally (or continues to be) at fault.

Regardless of the merits or faults present in each situation, it's not okay for us to inflict emotional pain on one another. That should be a basic tenet.

A commitment to compassion and justice and against cruelty (yes, that's what it is) needs to be overtly stated as the basis for how an egalitarian group operates.

We only need to look at the current political situation to see the wages of indifference and casual acceptance of cruelty. Once we have relinquished our moral compass, we can condone both small and huge moral insults with logical arguments and pragmatism. In the early years of the current war, where was the outrage of the American public at the deaths and injuries of Iraqi civilians? Even for those who believed the war to be politically justified, how could ecstatic cheering be the overwhelming reaction to death, suffering and destruction on a massive scale? Wouldn't the more human reaction be sober regretfulness that sometimes harm is done in order to achieve a purportedly worthwhile objective?

The purpose of activism, fundamentally, is to create a better world, one where there is greater justice, equality, and harmony and less pain and hardship. It is not to put forward a particular agenda. When we overlook this basic truth and allow ourselves to act with deliberate cruelty toward people in our own collectives, then go on to justify our actions by saying that we vilified or attacked our comrades because they were interfering with important political organizing, we have twisted our motives into an indefensible moral pretzel.

THE COLLECTIVE IS NOT ALWAYS MORE CORRECT THAN THE INDIVIDUAL

ONE MISTAKE OFTEN made by people who want to strive for a more equal society is to assume that the collective can always be trusted above the individual. Unfortunately, in many radical-left circles, if we talk too much about individual rights and even suggest that an individual's opinions and observations might be closer to the truth than the votes or consensus of the collective, we might be accused of pushing "individualism," which supposedly is a bad trait typical of "bourgeois" society, not to be tolerated in egalitarian circles. Yet, this kind of mentality, at least when taken to the extreme, enabled a lot of really nasty totalitarian societies to exist in the past century, and the history of those societies basically proves the point that individuals (who were suppressed) can often be more correct than the group.

If we are really striving for a fair and egalitarian society, then we need to give utmost importance to the rights and liberties of the individual. This does not mean promoting the kind of "individualism" that dictates that each person must look out for her/himself and that collective decision making and concern for the community are a hindrance to true liberty. What it does mean is that each of us is unique and must be considered, judged, and observed according to our own unique combination of circumstances. This means that our behaviors are far more complex than might be assumed by the knee-jerk sort of ideologue who would say, for instance, that any of us enjoys certain privileges above others for belonging to one particular group based on race, gender, or ethnic origins. It also means that nobody's behavior should be judged by a formulaic checklist, so that in any given situation, one person must be assumed to have certain politically undesirable characteristics based on a particular incident when we don't know the backgrounds, tendencies, or histories of the individuals involved. (So, for example, a man who shouts at a woman or says something vaguely disrespectful to her is automatically assumed to be "sexist" when a closer examination of the histories of the individuals involved might reveal a dynamic that is far more complex, with more equal hostilities, etc., than anyone realized.) When we fail to recognize the potential uniqueness and complexity of the individual, then we are failing to create a situation in which each individual might enjoy a maximum amount of freedom and liberty.

Sometimes, moreover, the individual can be very badly misunderstood by a group which has made assumptions or followed presumptions that might not really apply to the person involved. In judging individuals, groups can make terrible mistakes, sometimes based on unexamined bias and prejudice. This is illustrated not only by the countless collectivist mistakes made throughout history, but also by the many smaller examples of collective injustice and manipulation that we have already discussed in this book. When a group is manipulated, becomes misguided, or simply fails to be vigilant about judging everyone fairly and equally, it can become more wrong than any single member.

The individual also might have a particular outlook or opinion in a given situation that ultimately proves to be wiser or more accurate than the outlook of the group. This is why it really is necessary to listen to the opinions of individuals within the group who may not be going so well with the collective flow. Dissenting opinions some-times can change the mind of the entire group, once the group considers the dissenting opinion fairly, allowing each person within that group to weigh the merits of each (differing) point of view.

In examining other literature dealing with problems within collectives, we have seen quite a few articles talk-ing about how to deal with the difficult person who won't go along with the group, the ornery person, the mal-content whose behavior or opinions seem to disrupt the group's smooth functioning. The issue is thus usually de-picted as finding a good way for the group to collectively deal with a problem member. Unfortunately, this is only one way of looking at things.

A truly democratic and egalitarian collective can't always assume that the only problem to be considered in group-versus-individual conflicts is protecting the integrity of the group against the disruptive individual. Sometimes, the problem involves protecting the individ-ual against the group.

MAKING IT WORK

FOR NEWCOMERS

IN MAINSTREAM SOCIETY, we usually have to wait for someone to give us permission or acknowledge our worth before we can contribute our skills and ideas to a project. Anyone who has been grilled and scrutinized at a job interview knows that first hand. An egalitarian collective, by definition, presupposes that we each have something to offer and that everyone's contribution is valuable.

A newcomer won't necessarily feel instantly at ease (collectives have a tendency to have their own internal culture that has developed over time), but most collectives are very happy to see new members who want to offer their help. One of the most rewarding aspects of working in a collective is the sense of community. Very often (uhm, notwithstanding what you've read here...) collectives have an easy, relaxed camaraderie. The fundamental egalitarian belief that everyone has a place in the world means that egalitarian groups will accept a new face easily, as matter of course, without prejudging anyone and without applying some predetermined assessment of fitness. It's then up to the individual to live up to that initial trust through her actions.

It may take a little time to figure out the unspoken rules, the climate, and the general expectations of the collective. Some collectives may be strict about following protocols that will be unfamiliar at first, or that might even seem obtuse, while others may have little patience for process sticklers and may function much more organically. Some groups will welcome initiative, while others may frown when someone takes on tasks or initiates projects without following some particular procedure. A good first step might be simply to ask what help is needed.

This book outlines some of the difficulties that can crop up in collectives. A newbie probably won't be in a position to directly address possible squabbles or power plays, even if she can perhaps see them most clearly as an outsider. We don't recommend sticking one's neck out to tackle difficult issues right off the bat—or ever, if the major players in the collective have developed entrenched positions of unacknowledged power; otherwise, the poor hapless newcomer may find herself unhappily referring to the chapter on creating pariahs and painfully recognizing herself in its pages. But anyone can help ensure the health of the group by refraining from jumping to conclusions or giving credence to baseless rumors, and by being the level head who is willing to listen to all sides.

If you have a genuine desire to be helpful and productive, you will almost always be appreciated. Collectives are often strapped for time, resources, and people, so anyone willing to contribute will likely find that it's not difficult to become an integral part of the group.

FOR OLD-SCHOOLERS

In many cases, people who are old hands at collectives have developed a particular style that works for them. But collectives tend to be in constant flux, and old habits may need reexamining from time to time. Within a given group, there's usually a core of volunteers or workers who have taken on the lion's share of the group's daily functions.

That can be a comfortable arrangement, but a truly egalitarian collective makes room for newer members. In other words, new members should be kept adequately informed and be allowed to participate in discussions, contribute ideas, and ask questions. They might be in the best position to see old, unproductive habits for what they are. And as they contribute their own fresh knowledge and style, the collective will grow organically.

It's not unusual for small collectives, or their core membership, to become cliquish. It might be fun sometimes to tell old stories (and stories at the expense of past members are especially fun...), but that sort of behavior can turn newer members off. When influential or longstanding members display a particular style—such as a predilection for sarcasm—or make frequent references to inside jokes that only the core of the membership can share in, this can become ingrained as the culture of the collective. Newcomers can feel lost or intimidated. They might sense that they are unwelcome, or, at the very least, that they had better get with the program if they have any hope of fitting in. This creates a sort of closed loop: an exclusionary culture is cemented into place, even though nobody intended or wished for such a thing to happen.

A collective should look somewhat outward, rather than getting stuck in its own little world (or little history). It may be easier to fall back on familiar patterns than it is to try new things, but that can be a recipe for stagnation. Even worse, if the collective is not willing to admit past mistakes, it could continue on a negative path, alienating or dividing its members.

Longstanding members are usually in the best position to address problems when they crop up. This is especially true if they have gained respect for their many contributions. But they also have a particular responsibility to remain vigilant about negative dynamics, offering their considered judgment and listening to all sides carefully. It can be harder to keep a level head when one is deep on the inside of a conflict, but that involvement should not result in bias. Personal loyalties must not take second place to the principle of fairness towards all.

Experienced members are also in the best position to create a legacy. The collective must be able to thrive as its membership changes. If the experienced members share their skills and knowledge, that collective will be able to continue even after a highly valued member leaves. A collective can't remain healthy in the long term if it depends too much on the contributions of any one person.

RELINQUISHING CONTROL

THE EGALITARIAN GROUP affords its members little opportunity to control other members or the group itself. Because there are no leaders, no one is in a position to force another person to act or refrain from acting in a given situation; only the collective as a whole can intervene, and then it should be only to limit unprincipled behavior. Since the entire collective has to become involved in order to restrict someone's autonomy, such a measure should be undertaken only if the behavior in question is extreme. (We have seen many instances in which small gaffes are trumped up into serious charges as a way of exercising control, but that's another topic, discussed elsewhere.) In any collective, we are likely to encounter some people who have annoying quirks, others who are chatterboxes, and others who just don't think before proposing stupid ideas. But these are not the egregious kinds of behaviors that require official control. Galling as they might seem at times, they must be allowed to exist. (The corollary to this is that group members have a responsibility not to make themselves a nuisance to others.)

When a collective member tries to force a desired outcome according to her personal wishes, she is basically violating the principles of maximum autonomy and free choice. This tendency will almost always lead to arguments and ruffled feelings. (Note, however, that someone making a principled objection can sometimes be accused of expressing a personal peeve, since that is a standard way to discredit an opponent in a debate.) A truly egalitarian collective will likely not be smooth or harmonious—though it may be loving and collegial—but highly heterogeneous, rife with rough spots and bumps.

In an egalitarian group, not everybody has to agree or like each other, or approve of the work that is being done: they merely have to consent to it. This means that unless something is really important or central to the values of the organization, the wisest course is often just to let things be. That can be hard to accept when we have been accustomed to value results over all other considerations.

Almost all people who come to the movement for social justice were brought up and have been functioning in conventional society, which presupposes supremacy of one person over another according to status or perceived superior ability. Whether we mean to or not, we bring these biases and expectations with us when we join groups that operate according to equality and collectivism.

Those who are accustomed to emerging as natural leaders (for instance, those who've been successful in academia) may have an unacknowledged belief that others will readily recognize their wisdom and defer to it as a matter of course. We may assume that, egalitarian goals notwithstanding, the opinions of people who have distinguished themselves in some way will naturally carry more weight. Or we may become concerned that the outcome of the group's work will not be of the high caliber that we ourselves feel capable of achieving. Others among us may readily accede to individuals who seem knowledgeable and capable of taking on challenging problems, and may even frown on those who don't allow themselves to be molded, further alienating individuals who challenge the leadership.

Many conflicts arise out of the desire to control other people's behavior and to control the output of the group's activities. Whenever an attempt is made to manage or direct another member of the group, no matter how well meaning (to preserve harmony, end disruption, make time to tend to the work of the group, ensure high quality, etc.), that person will inevitably feel resentful, and possibly very hurt or angry. If she reacts, conflict begins. Many conflicts that drag down collectives for months, often resulting in indelible feuds, could have been prevented if the collective's members were more willing to tolerate the coexistence of different opinions, approaches or strategies, objecting only when a fundamental principle was at stake.

A longtime volunteer may bristle at the possibility that a newcomer has as much say about a group and projects that he himself helped build with his sweat, maybe for years, but the issue here is not recognition of individual contributions, it's what will produce the best outcomes for the group and its work while maintaining its adherence to core values. Although some people might have a tough time accepting this, collectives are not meritocracies.

The end result of a project that has been produced collectively is an uneven patchwork of viewpoints and ability levels. Making room for everybody to contribute, even when ability is not equal, is a strength, not a weakness; so is letting the process show. We are accustomed to valuing a slick, polished presentation, but if we let the seams show, this will empower others with information about how something was put together. If we accept a heterogeneous, bumpy outcome as a given, before the work even begins, we will avoid a lot of head-butting further down the road.

Because groups based on equality presuppose mutual trust and a shared sense of mission, many of us may expect solidarity, harmony, and kindness to permeate such groups. On the contrary, adhering to egalitarian, anti-authoritarian principles means applying minimal interference to one another, or letting people be who they are—including the annoying, the trying, and the obnoxious—and accepting the outcomes as well.

STAYING TRUE TO THE MISSION

MANY EGALITARIAN COLLECTIVES consist of activists working to achieve a just society and were formed for that purpose. Even collectives that don't have specific political aims have made a commitment to social justice by virtue of being anti-authoritarian and pursuing equality as a fundamental goal. It should be obvious that internal power plays, deceitful back-room plotting, rumor mongering, and marginalizing or ridiculing are behaviors that do not befit a group fighting for fairness and against oppression. Yet, people in collectives do these things all the time, and usually without even inviting a raised eyebrow.

Collectives that incorporate as nonprofits are required by law to draft a mission statement letting potential supporters know about the work that the organization exists to achieve. Fulfilling the mission is a nonprofit's legal reason for being (as well as the reason it doesn't have to pay taxes), just as a for-profit company's all-consuming purpose is to make money for its owners. Most collectives have no such mandated requirement, but it's still a good idea to compose a mission statement to refer back to whenever a decision needs to be made on how the group should act in a given situation. This position paper should spell out the fundamental belief that the collective must operate internally by the same high standards of fairness and democracy that it is working to bring about in the larger society. If it fails to do that, then it has failed in its most basic goal.

WHAT'S A LONE PERSON TO DO?

IF YOU'RE READING this book because you see a problem in your collective that you think should be addressed, you may well be alone in your quest. If you've actually raised your concerns with the group, you may suddenly find yourself the outcast, with the rest of the members possibly either openly hostile or utterly indifferent.

It's all well and good to say that all the people in a collective need to take responsibility for the group's

operation in order to avoid power inequalities and ensure a true spirit of collectivity, but if you're just one
person, and the group is in fact not taking responsibility
and is allowing a self-appointed leader or faction to steer
decisions (including the newly arrived at conclusion that
perhaps you are no longer a valued or wanted member),
what can you, alone, do?

We wish we had the answer. This chapter is more
than anything a cautionary note. Because you have read
the contents of this book (and hopefully a number of
others) on the topic of collective function and dysfunc-
tion, you may consider yourself armed with an arsenal
of information and insight on what is going wrong with
your group. You may feel confident that you can make
a good case to the membership for the need for self
analysis and reassessment of priorities. But that doesn't
mean you won't still find yourself alone and the subject
of attacks and slander.

Evidence from books is very unconvincing to people
who won't make an effort to try to understand the situation or the underlying problems, and even less so to
anyone who has already reached a conclusion based on
rumors, speculation, and innuendos. There is a saying,
which unfortunately is all too often appropriate in collectives that are experiencing conflict: "My mind is made
up, don't bother me with facts."

In many cases, people who feel they have carved out
their little corner of power are not going to give it up
easily, no matter how trivial their sphere of influence
may seem. If you threaten the hegemony of someone in
a position of some authority, whether his leadership is
overt or subtle, (or even if you haven't done anything that

could be construed as a threat but he thinks there's the potential that you might, perhaps because you've been outspoken) you may very well see another side of him, one with bared teeth and hissing.

It has been suggested that rather than going it alone one should set out to build a coalition, persuading each person individually, through private conversation, before making one's concerns public. This is classic political strategizing. We feel very ambivalent about this. On the one hand, it might work, and it could be preferable to exposing oneself as a sole target to a verbal battering. On the other hand, it's a manipulative tactic that could be characterized as sleazy, depending on the amount and quality of the persuasion involved.

Furthermore, you will always be out-sleazed by the other party if she is willing to go further than you are. This is not a competition worth entering into unless you're willing to go over to the dark side. After your fellow collective members have figuratively beaten you up with personal attacks, vilification, and calls for your banishment, we think you will want, at least, to walk away with your integrity.

THIS COULDN'T HAPPEN IN OUR COLLECTIVE

In reading these chapters, members of a collective that is friendly and collegial, and who feel a genuine sense of community and shared effort within their group, may think that these issues don't apply to them. If you're lucky, there is, indeed, a chance that your group might never have to contend with such concerns.

But the nature of collectives is that they are constantly in flux. Assuming that a given collective doesn't have to pay attention to process because "We feel we can trust each other and none of us are going to do any of these dastardly things you describe" could be a recipe for future disaster. We're not suggesting you should become paranoid or mistrustful. Our recommendation is just that you seek clarity: establish and write down the basic principles and guidelines that your group will operate by so that you are not suddenly blindsided by an unexpected breakdown in group dynamics without any compass to help steer the collective back on course. And remain vigilant for the red flags we have outlined here.

It is much more difficult to deal with power imbalances and underhanded or authoritarian tactics once they've already been established and have taken hold. Sometimes, in fact, it becomes impossible. Anyone who brings up the issue once it already exists is likely to be cast as a malcontent or troublemaker; then he might find himself the target of hatred and vilification. The best, and perhaps only, way to stop this kind of manipulation of the collective process is through prevention.

GETTING THINGS DONE

BECAUSE THIS IS a book about collective process, it may give the impression that we are advocating that collective members should do nothing else but pay attention to process, or that they should sit through endless meetings at which people air their grievances, engage in conflict resolution, and discuss power sharing.

That is not what we are advocating. In fact, when we spend too much time on procedural issues or on addressing people's complaints and their perceptions of having been slighted, that can become very tiresome.

Sometimes it can even be a reason why people become fed up with their participation in collectives. We are suggesting, instead, that fair dealing and transparency should simply be built into the process of the collective. These matters do not have to be discussed ad nauseum. The process needs to be agreed upon, written down, and put into use as a day-to-day protocol that is always present in the active mindfulness of the collective's members. This will serve to ensure that an underlying framework of clarity and trust is the basis on which the collective's functioning is predicated.

SOME CARDINAL POINTS TO KEEP IN MIND WHEN CONFLICT ARISES:

1. Do not draw any conclusions about an issue without hearing from both sides. Hear each side out to the extent that each feels is necessary (i.e., don't assume you've heard enough just because someone seems tiresome, pedantic, or emotional). Talking to a friend of a person involved in a conflict is not the same as getting the lowdown straight from the horse's mouth.

2. Although you may feel it is your duty to throw your support behind a friend or close ally who is in distress, giving emotional support is possible—and desirable—without having to draw conclusions or take sides.

3. Corollary to #2. Regardless of who you believe is right or wrong on a given issue, give emotional support. It is not okay for the feelings of the people involved to be trampled on, especially if someone is clearly suffering, even when one or both of the parties are acting like jerks. It is

especially not okay to jump in and join the faction doing the stomping on someone's hurt feelings.

4. Assume that every concern is legitimate and address its substance, even if the tone or context in which it is delivered seems overblown, emotional, or vindictive.

5. Corollary to #4. Do not dismiss concerns just because the manner in which they are brought up seems strident or out of place. It is one of the shameful practices of the adversarial court system, which we don't want to emulate in our own collectives (at least not in this respect), to discredit complainants who are emotional or enraged. For centuries, women's grievances, in particular, have been successfully shunted aside by overbearing men by claiming that a woman who is outraged to the breaking point by the injustices and abuses she has had to suffer is hysterical. (Keep in mind that men can be very emotional too, and just as readily dismissed for being so.)

6. Never assume that someone who is raising a concern is just wasting the group's time. (That can happen, of course, but, at worst, the outcome of such a situation will simply be a certain amount of time wasted.) Much more often, someone who feels threatened by the concern raised will try to persuade the group to squelch it on the grounds that it is a time-waster.

7. If a concern is in fact taking up too much of the group's time, create a subcommittee to look into it. The subcommittee should include the person raising

the concern and at least three other people who are neutral or uninvolved in the issue but who are willing to take the time to ferret out the facts and study them thoroughly.

8. Sometimes someone (or a group) can be so controlling or self-involved (often without even realizing it) that he sees any disagreement with his chosen course as sabotage or disruption and will react angrily to what he sees as an unnecessary obstacle being created. This is a very common source of conflict in collectives. The solution is to treat every concern that is raised as legitimate and to address it as such. There are often fundamental differences in the basic values or beliefs of group members that get swept under the rug in a flurry of angry accusations and are only brought to an end by driving out or expelling the weaker faction or individual. This is a terrible breakdown of collectivity and should never be viewed as a successful resolution to a conflict.

9. Be the solution. Volunteer to create a committee to look into a problem and, after thorough study, recommend solutions. Volunteer to seek outside mediators. Talk to both sides to try to understand each point of view.

10. Instead of listening to empty accusations, look for plausible motives for people's behavior. When someone is accused of acting a certain way because he is "crazy," that just does not hold any water. People usually act badly either because they are upset, insecure,

frustrated, or afraid, or because they have something to gain by that behavior. Why would someone who has nothing to gain go around sabotaging or undermining the group's work? Could it be that they in fact have a legitimate concern they feel needs to be raised and are only being painted as saboteurs by someone who in fact has something to gain (such as consolidating his own power) by shutting them up?

11. A solution to a conflict does not have to—and should not—assign blame nor declare a victor. When conflicts arise, emotions often run high. People who feel they have been wronged or mistreated can react badly. Often, one side (or both) has become so overwrought by the conflict that she does not want to resolve the problem but merely crush the perceived offender. It is necessary to create an atmosphere where both sides can come back to the group relatively whole. That can only happen when all the issues have been thoroughly addressed and resolved to an extent that both parties can live with.

12. Not assigning blame does not mean not acknowledging the wrongs that have been visited on either side. When people are not made to feel that they are under attack, but that their concerns will be genuinely listened to, they are much more likely to admit their mistakes. Create a means for people who may have acted badly to make amends, so that everybody can move on. (But do not be the judge and jury. People can honestly make amends only for errors that they acknowledge. No one can be forced to admit she was

wrong if she does not in fact believe it. It may be that someone who is adamant in her position is in fact correct in her claim that she has been unjustly vilified. A situation that is still in this stage has not been thoroughly dealt with yet.)

13. A conflict between two people who were previously close friends or have been involved in a romantic relationship should never result in the group taking sides against one or the other party. The facts of the conflict that involve the group as a whole should be addressed as such (i.e., s/he has been excluding me from activities; badmouthing me within the group; will not leave me alone when I am doing work for the group, etc.). The group should absolutely not become complicit in eliminating the former friend or partner from the complainant's life by driving him or her out of the collective. It should become especially obvious in such a case why assigning blame is fruitless: people who have been hurt sometimes do stupid or cruel things. There's no need to rub their faces in it.

14. People become involved in conflicts because they have some unaddressed need. Find out what the need is and determine a way to address it, with the collaboration of those who are in disagreement. That is the only way to resolve the conflict: it needs to be addressed, worked through, and straightened out.

15. Anytime someone is kicked out of the group or leaves voluntarily in order to stop a painful conflict, there has been a terrible breakdown, not a conflict resolution.

CODIFYING THE COLLECTIVE PROCESS

IT'S TOO LATE to try to decide on a fair way of resolving an issue once the shit has already hit the fan. Whenever there's a problem within a collective, whether it involves back-and-forth accusations of wrongdoing, factional splits, or fundamental disagreements, emotions run high. This is not the time to decide on proper procedures. When people are already angry at someone or some group, they're often all too happy to just let the person(s) fry, process be damned.

That's why it's paramount that the collective have a set of procedural guidelines in place that can be referred to when difficulties crop up. Here, we offer a few suggestions to start with, but please keep in mind that it's up to each group to determine what they might find appropriate.

1. A Statement of Guiding Principles or Mission

This should form the basis to inform all other decisions.

Ideally, the mission statement should not be too prescriptive or narrow. For instance, including statements like "All members will treat each other with respect at all times" may sound good on its face but doesn't take into account the reality that people may sometimes lose their temper or their patience and should not, as a result, have to face the accusation of having violated a basic tenet.

On the other hand, a guiding statement should include the seemingly obvious, since in times of crisis common sense and common decency are often among the first casualties. It may be useful to overtly state that the group supports ideals such as kindness, equality, fairness, and openness while opposing bullying, lack of transparency, lying and manipulation.

With such a statement in place, it won't be as easy for a faction or individual to hijack the group's thinking or opinions whenever problems arise. It will be harder for someone to claim to be acting in the collective's best interest when her behavior is clearly at odds with the group's fundamental mission and principles.

There's a fine line here, however. A manipulative person can use the basic tenets codified in the mission statement as a weapon to attack a dissenter or someone he sees as a threat. To prevent this, the group may want to state explicitly that the mission statement is meant to guide the collective as a whole; it is not meant to be used as a prescription for individual behavior, nor, especially, a tool for sanction and punishment.

2. A Definition of Membership

This often becomes a tough issue, especially when a group is in crisis: who gets to have a say? Who gets to make a proposal? Who gets to vote on or object to a collective decision?

The question to ask is: how should decisions be made so that they are least likely to result in some part of the group being manipulated or silenced, or a more powerful person or faction getting their way in an underhanded manner?

If the collective lets newcomers or relative outsiders have a say in its work, that should limit cronyism. But sometimes newcomers who don't know the history of certain issues are the ones who fall prey most easily to manipulation by persuasive individuals or more senior members. A manipulative person might also seek specifically to bring in "plants" (people who are there just to shore up his position).

Generally, we recommend erring on the side of openness. As members of collectives committed to egalitarianism, we want to believe that everyone's input is valuable and that everyone has something to contribute. Many collectives find it useful to stipulate that anyone who has been volunteering for a given amount of time, say a month, is considered a member of the collective.

It may also be useful to ask: who has a stake in the success of our group's work? When establishing the guidelines on who gets to have a say, everyone who fits that category might be considered as a potential voting member.

3. A Decision-Making Procedure

This should be fairly cut-and-dry. It may be stipulated, for instance, whether decisions must be unanimous, or by two thirds majority, or whatever other manner the collective deems appropriate, and whether a certain percentage of the membership must be present for important decisions to pass. (Some definition of "important decision" might also be included.)

4. A Grievance Procedure

Grievances are slightly different from requests for conflict resolution since there may be only be one side that perceives a problem, but in either case, the procedure for resolving the problem can be the same.

It is imperative that grievances be heard by an unbiased, outside observer, or a panel made up of people *who are not members of the collective where the problem originated*. We cannot stress this enough. In a small group it's extraordinarily easy for rumors to spread quickly and biased opinions to solidify instantly.

We recommend that a collective establish a grievance committee, whose job it is to maintain a contact list of outside volunteers who are not, and have never been, members of the collective and who can be called in when needed.

The outside volunteers can hear the grievance and make recommendations for how to resolve it. If the recommendations include some action to be taken by the collective, then the collective must agree by consensus (or by the voting process established by that collective) on the action to take. Since the aggrieved person(s) are part of the collective, as are those against whom their grievance is directed, *neither side should be excluded* from this decision-making process. If an aggrieved member has been intimidated by the hostility of his detractor(s) and general disapproval of the collective, he may be too afraid to speak up or even attend the collective meeting, but a decision cannot be valid if it's made in his absence or without his input.

In many cases, the aggrieved will wish only to have their grievance heard and their concerns acknowledged and may not require any action on the part of the collective. It's possible also that the outside volunteers will determine that the grievance is frivolous or without merit and, if so, will reflect this in their recommendations.

5. Nuts and Bolts

Basic guidelines should not be subject to alteration on the whims of whoever is around at a given time, nor should they be based on the personalities who are active in the group at the time that they are drafted. For instance, even if the group trusts the current treasurer, it should not ignore the need to lay down basic accounting guidelines. The same holds true for other areas.

THERE'S HOPE

VIRTUALLY ALL PROBLEMS in collectives can be overcome by applying compassion, and by being thorough and even-handed in our thinking.

Recognize that some people are a big pain in the ass, but that doesn't mean that they are agent provocateurs. And even if they are, the best way to deal with disruptors in either case is probably to give them a certain amount of leeway to be themselves, to let them carry on instead of demanding that they cease. Provocation can be defused simply by not engaging it.

If the level of annoyance is such that it cannot simply be tolerated, then talk it over with the person: let him know what behaviors of his are causing problems for you and help him find ways to change them. Actions that we may see as negative usually arise from a need on the part of the person engaging in them: whether it's the need to be listened to, to get to the bottom of issues, etc. Our job is to help find a way for the person to still be able to have his need met if he agrees to drop the offending behavior. The only way to do that is to talk to him. People who are being a nuisance don't see themselves that way. They have a reason for what they're doing. Try to learn their perspective. Some people act in bad faith. Learn their perspective too, so you can expose it for what it is.

If we care, genuinely, about mutuality and inclusion, if we believe this to be one of the basic reasons why we want to work for a better, more just world, then we need to ask ourselves a simple question: if this person whom we cannot stand were a member of our family, would we turn her out into the street? Or would we put our hearts ahead of our frayed nerves and learn to deal with her annoying character traits? Likewise, if a member of our family spoke frankly and unkindly to us ("Look, you're driving me nuts: could you please just shut up?"), would we demand that the whole family intervene to sanction her?

Because most of us tend to throw caution or our sense of fairness to the wind whenever someone has made us very angry, we recommend having clear and concrete protocols in place that can be called upon whenever conflicts, differences in approach, or hurt feelings crop up. Rules, however, though they can help us keep our priorities in order, cannot take the place of basic human qualities: compassion, patience, tolerance, and the desire to seek out the truth. Without our humanity as our foremost guiding principle, no set of guidelines can come to our rescue. We need to always keep referring back to what's important when striving to make decisions on how to proceed, especially in a difficult or trying situation. What's important is not the work of the group nor effecting political change: it's the fact that we care about and value one another, as we do all people. That's why we're in the struggle for social justice, after all.

Some groups may have no patience for tending to the weak and the whiny. They may feel that those who do not contribute or are slowing or bringing the rest of the collective down need to move on and get out of the way. Any group can choose that path, of course. But if they do, they have a responsibility to do so honestly and openly. Such an enterprise can no longer call itself egalitarian.